How to Talk Minnesotan

As a writer for *A Prairie Home Companion* in its early years, Howard Mohr created over two hundred scripts and ad spots, including RAW BITS ("the tough natural cereal made from oat hulls and wheat chaff"); POLKA PANTS ("available at fine accordion stores everywhere—they don't blow out under stress"); BIGGER HAMMER HARDWARE ("just as helpful as your next-door neighbor, but without all that sarcasm that hurts so much"); SLOW-DECAY SNACK CAKES ("they'll last longer than you will"); THE COLLEGE OF LOW-TECHNOLOGY; WORST CASE SCENARIO; and ONE-MINUTE RO-MANCES ("sponsored by PORK BRAND SHOES—they squeak a little but they don't sweat"). Howard frequently appeared on *A Prairie Home Companion* in his own material as Howie Humde (owner of the WALLEYE PHONE COMPANY, "two-way service by request only"); as Herb (of HERB'S ACU-AUTO, "the Midwest's only acupuncture garage"); and as Bob Humde (inventor of the COW PIE KEY HIDER).

Howard's long-running "commercials" on *A Prairie Home Companion* for Minnesota Language Systems ("the simple cassette tape and study guide for visitors from out of state, so they don't stick out like a sore thumb") became the heart of his best-selling book *How to Talk Minnesotan*.

In January 1997 Howard's musical version of *How to Talk Minnesotan* opened to a five-year run at the Plymouth Playhouse. On January 29, 2010, the show opened once again at the playhouse for a run through October.

Howard has also written *A Minnesota Book of Days (And a Few Nights)*. *Book of Days* features his friend Harold Mire, who—like the author—probably spends too much time tinkering with old cars and collecting stuff that might be useful someday.

After the publication of *How to Talk Minnesotan* in 1987, Howard was frequently asked to do "speaking engagements" for groups as diverse as the Minnesota Beef Council and the International Association of Building Code Inspectors.

In 1992 a half-hour video version of *How to Talk Minnesotan* was produced and directed by John Whitehead for Twin Cities Public Television and won a regional Emmy in Chicago for Best Single Entertainment Show in October 1992. The video was partly filmed in and around Cottonwood and stars many of Howard's friends and neighbors.

Howard and his wife live on five acres of southwestern Minnesota prairie, where all 360 degrees of the horizon can be clearly seen and studied, and where a rusty '46 Dodge pickup stares at them through the kitchen window from its permanent parking spot at the edge of the grove, a memorial to Howard's father, a mechanic and truck driver.

The Mohrs have two outdoor cats, and just about the right number of possums, skunks, groundhogs, and coyotes. Visitors from the big city always ask, "What do you do out here for fun?" And Howard says, "This is it. You're doing it now."

Also by Howard Mohr

How to Tell a Tornado
A Minnesota Book of Days (And a Few Nights)

How to Talk Minnesotan

Revised for the 21st Century

Howard Mohr

PENGUIN BOOKS

PENGUIN BOOKS
Published by the Penguin Group
Penguin Group (USA) Inc., 375 Hudson Street,
New York, New York 10014, USA

USA | Canada | UK | Ireland | Australia | New Zealand | India | South Africa | China
Penguin Books Ltd, Registered Offices: 80 Strand, London WC2R 0RL, England
For more information about the Penguin Group visit penguin.com

First published in Penguin Books 1987
This revised edition published 2013

A somewhat different version of "Winter Vacations in Minnesota" was published as "How
to Ice Fish Like a Minnesotan" in *No Boundaries*, a Ford Motor Company magazine.

Other portions of this book first appeared, some in different form, in *City Pages, Milkweed
Chronicle, Mpls. St. Paul* magazine, *Minnesota Monthly*, and *St. Paul Pioneer Press*.

Selected portions of "Minnesota Language System" were originally heard on "A Prairie
Home Companion," produced by Minnesota Public Radio.

LIBRARY OF CONGRESS CATALOGING-IN-PUBLICATION DATA
Mohr, Howard.
How to Talk Minnesotan : Revised for the 21st century /
Howard Mohr.—Revised [edition]
pages cm
ISBN 978-0-14-312269-2
1. English language—Dialects—Minnesota.   2. English language—Minnesota—
Humor.   3. English language—History—21st century.   4. Americanisms—
Minnesota.   5. Minnesota—Languages.   I. Title.
PE3101.M6M64 2013
427'.97760207—dc23
2012044291

Printed in the United States of America
3   5   7   9   10   8   6   4   2

Set in Sabon
Designed by Spring Hoteling

To Jody, Susan, and Jackson

HOW TO TALK MINNESOTAN
IN THE TWENTY-FIRST CENTURY

My certified birth name is Howard Henry Mohr. Many times over the twenty-five years since the publication of *How to Talk Minnesotan*, when I have been introduced to strangers, especially Minnesotans, it is not unusual for them to say after a momentary pause, "You're the guy who wrote that book." I am fond of that tag, as you can imagine. The visitor's guide has been popular and is still in print in 2012, which is why, on this silver anniversary of publication, Penguin has assigned me the task of updating "that book."

My editor's idea is to bring *How to Talk Minnesotan* into the twenty-first century, a fairly good idea, since a lot has happened in the world since 1987. The potential problem was that the guy who wrote that book had not brought himself into the twenty-first century yet—well, maybe a little, say 33 percent. I look at 1987, and it stands out as a harmless sort of year in a century that had some very good points. Is it just me? The twenty-first century so far has been science fiction. Take banks for example. In the twentieth century they were uppity, tight, and extremely proud of themselves, but they rarely slapped you upside the head when you asked for a loan. When I put 2012 as the year on a check I write, I just figure the bank will send it back with a note: "Listen, Buster, get Captain Kirk to cash it for you. Don't try this again. We value your privacy but we know everything about you and have no reason not to publish it if you don't shape up. How's your hernia, by the way?"

I may be wrong, but I have it in my head that readers old and new might like to know about the origin of *How to Talk Minnesotan*.

In 1985 I was already well into writing comedy for *A Prairie Home Companion* (*APHC*) on a weekly basis, often performing in my scripts and spots. I wrote many ads for strange products, including "RAW BITS, the tough natural cereal made from oat hulls and wheat chaff. It's not for everybody."

In the meantime my wife and teenage daughter and I were planning to visit friends in Germany that summer, and all three of us were brushing up on minimal German. Jody and Susan were driving to town for groceries on a spring day, practicing handy phrases from a guide for English visitors. They broke up laughing when they got to "Wie viel kostet die Bratwurst?" and kept repeating it. Jody's foot was a bit heavy for the patrolman who stopped them. She got a warning for ten miles per hour over, and I got some material from it: Hey! Why not write a visitor's guide for Minnesota?

I started by writing "Minnesota Language Systems" (MLS) ads one at a time for *APHC*. I did twenty-six of the MLS spots all told. Garrison Keillor introduced the ads with "This portion of the show brought to you by 'Minnesota Language Systems,' the simple cassette tape and study guide for people from out of state." I would write in a person from a foreign place, such as New York City or California, who said a phrase wrong, and then I spoke Minnesotan to correct the error. The lesson closed with "Minnesota Language Systems. After a few weeks of study, you will think you've lived in Minnesota all your life, and so will your mom." I wrote the first "Minnesota Language Systems" spot early in 1985.

In the fall of 1985 I got a call from Garrison's literary agent in New York City, who proceeded to tell me that she had received a call from a publisher who wanted Garrison to turn those "Minnesota Language Systems" spots into a book they would publish. She said she called Garrison, and he informed her that he did not write those. Howard wrote them. No surprise that nobody knew I wrote them. I was rarely mentioned as a writer on the show, except in a goofy way, as "Manuel Transmission" for example. I grew up on radio, especially radio comedy, and to have a comedy writing job on radio in the 1980s was quite the deal. It was all great fun while it lasted.

I sent the manuscript for *How to Talk Minnesotan* to Viking/Penguin in September 1986, and it was in the bookstores the summer of 1987.

Okay then, I have done my best on this update thing, which is all a guy can do sometimes.

—H.H.M.
2012

Foreword
by the Author's Mechanic

My yard is full of cars that I told my customers I'd get to immediately, if not sooner, but I cleaned the grease off my hands with Goop anyway and came in here and sat down at the kitchen table to do what I have to do. I'd rather be on my back under a car drilling out a rusted bolt on a steering knuckle—it would be more entertaining. I'm writing on the blank back of February and March off this year's tool calendar. I used to keep the old calenders for further study, but they stopped taking snapshots of good-looking women in tiny bathing suits and high heels lounging on trunk lids with a wrench in their hands. I suppose somebody threatened to sue or something—all of a sudden the tool company switched to covered bridges over creeks and sheep standing around in a pasture, which are okay to look at, but I don't consider them keepers.

The author of this book is a guy I've known for going on fifteen years, which means we've caught a few walleyes and bullheads together, and every summer there for a while we'd manage to get up to the Cities for a Twins game, back when they played outdoors at the Met stadium, which they tore down. My cousin salvaged one of the big lights for me and I welded it to an axle which I welded to a truck-tire rim for a base and rewired it for a worklight. Now they play in the Hubert H. Humphrey Metrodome. We tried one game there. I don't remember who was playing center field, but it made me dizzy and a little sick to my stomach to see that far and still be inside a building, but it could've been the flat beer, too, I don't know. I don't mind a cool one every so often— with a Brat—but what they were serving was warm ones in wax cups covered with Saran wrap. It tasted like if we sent a sample of it to the vet, he'd say our horse had diabetes.

Well, hats off to my friend on his book. I hope he makes enough money from it to buy a new car or a fairly good used one, because personally I don't think that Rambler of his should be on the road— and I'm known as a liberal when it comes to driving junkers. I've done everything I can for that Nash, short of faith healing. If it had been anybody else's car, I would have administered last rites at

172,000 after the carburetor exploded. It launched itself right through the hood and made a hole you could've passed a gallon jug of milk through, which he patched with chicken wire and tar paper to keep the rain out. It's an eyesore. It does start in the winter, though—mostly because it cranks over so easy, the compression is so low. The pistons just sort of rattle around in the cylinders. She burns a little oil and it takes about five minutes to go from 0 to 50 mph, but a good starter is worth its weight in gold, even without fenders or rear seats.

I will say that this book of his should stop some of the speculation about what he does all day, but whether it will improve his reputation in the community, we'll have to wait and see. For a couple of years, the UPS guys wouldn't deliver packages to his house, but his neighbors told them he was just an author and completely harmless no matter what he looked like when he came to the door. He's only got two sets of clothes. He wears one set till they can stand up by themselves, and then he switches to the other set, which is almost identical. But it takes all kinds, and he's right in there with the best of them.

I'm not sure everybody's gonna like this book as much as I do—and I don't mean to say it's the best book I've ever tried to read, but it's definitely in the average range, and if you keep at it, I think you can get through it without any trouble. Of course, I've been from Minnesota since I was born, so the book really isn't all that useful to me, but it's got to be helpful to visitors. I've seen some doozies. They come rolling into Minnesota with their eyes wide open and not the foggiest idea about where they are or what they're supposed to do while they're here. But if their car is broke, I fix it, same as anybody else's. We're all equal when it comes to cars. That's my philosophy.

Well, I'm at the bottom of March and I got three cars sitting out there I said would be done before five. One of them is Ted Mason's '78 Chevy, and if it doesn't run like new when he picks it up, I'll hear about it. The problem is, it didn't even run like new when he bought it new. If I can get it to run like a top, I'll be happy.

CONTENTS

Contents

Contents

Contents

A Twenty-fifth Anniversary Congratulatory Message from the Chair of the University of Minnesota's Widely Acclaimed MSL Program
(Minnesotan as a Second Language)

Mr. Mohr's book has been a staple in our Minnesotan as a Second Language Program for twenty-five years, helping thousands of visitors and new residents to our great state enjoy themselves after they adjust to and learn the language and culture of the Gopher State. And it goes without saying that every summer hordes of tourists from the far-flung parts of our nation arrive for a vacation at a fishing lodge on one of our legendary Ten Thousand Lakes. It is the rare lodge that does not have a tattered copy of *How to Talk Minnesotan* in each cabin. First-time visitors can, by absorbing just the first two lessons in the guide, talk Minnesotan with the lodge manager or fishing guide without too much embarrassment.

I personally am gratified to learn that the iconic *How to Talk Minnesotan* will be updated. Mr. Mohr hinted as much a year ago when he gave a lecture to our advanced MSL class on campus. He is provocative and, might I say, quite entertaining, in addition to being relentlessly factual and informative, adhering to the highest academic standards of scholarship and research.

We are especially pleased that one fishing lodge instituted Minnesota language lessons as part of its vacation packages. Lost Walleye Lodge on Leech Lake is owned and operated by the lovely down-to-earth family of Lucy and Ed Humde. Many of the lessons are set to music accompanied by The Muskie Three, a very popular local band, a favorite at hog roasts and Legion halls across northern Minnesota. Other lodges in the busy Leech Lake area often send their out-of-state guests over to Lost Walleye Lodge to brush up on Minnesotan.

As one would expect, tourists from afar returning to Minnesota's lake country summer after summer grow increasingly more fluent by studying the visitor's guide on a rainy day at the lodge, or making forays beyond the lodge to try out their Minnesotan at the casino or the sporting goods shops. A very unusual but gratifying phenomenon has developed in the larger lodges, where thirty cabins might have tourists from several states at the same time, and oddly enough, after a couple of days there, they all naturally revert to Minnesotan as the common language. Lodge guests from New Jersey or Maine, and even Texas, talk Minnesotan to each other so much that they have often been mistaken for Minnesotans after getting back home, where they take a good ribbing for it.

Minnesota companies by the dozens have inserted a copy of *How to Talk Minnesotan* into the employee packets of new hires from out of state who might have floundered for months, slowing down production and making themselves miserable, without the valuable advice provided in the guide.

I am happy to report that federal funding for the Minnesotan as a Second Language outreach program came through in late 2011, and we now offer fully accredited classes at the University of Wisconsin in Madison, Ole Miss, and UCLA. We are in the final phases of negotiations with the University of Iowa, Harvard, and MIT.

It is my pleasure in closing to include the following remarks by Jane and Jake Gratley, fully certified Minnesota marriage counselors, who can't say enough good about the value of Mr. Mohr's guide for struggling marriages.

"Marriage counselors in Minnesota frequently deal with UOS (unions on the skids), where women from such exotic areas as Chicago, New York, Los Angeles, and Atlanta, marry a Minnesota man and within a few months are throwing up their hands in frustration. Counselors have found that the union can be saved if the wife is given a copy of *How to Talk Minnesotan*. The Minnesota man is truly a complex species, though nice enough guys, really, who try to do their best to be better, not that they are all that bad. We have seen no other book that is as helpful to our main clientele."

—J & J Gratley

Once more, Mr. Mohr, congratulations and thank you for being you.

—Emmet C. Borde, PhD, Chair, MSL Program, U of M

How to Talk Minnesotan

Getting Started in Minnesotan

Handy Words and Phrases

✓ *You bet*
✓ *That's different*
✓ *Whatever*

These three workhorses of Minnesota conversation will carry you through your first scary hours here. Memorize them, work on them at home with your family, repeat them until they are second nature. They are the building blocks of all dialogue.

✓ *You Bet*

If you fly in, your first chance to try Minnesotan will likely occur at the airport:

—"We found your suitcase, it got caught in the conveyor belt. Some of your underwear fell out and was shredded by the pulley. Otherwise it's okay. We taped the handle back on, it should last you."

—"Oh, thanks."

—"You bet. But your dog is another matter. We think he's on the plane to Kansas City, but no problem, we'll find him."

—"I appreciate that."

—"You bet."

On the other hand, if you drive to Minnesota you could have car trouble right away and be towed to a gas station:

—"I don't like the sound of that thing. At first I thought maybe just moisture in the distributor cap, but now, I don't know, I think we're talking valves here, or a broken piston."

—"I appreciate your concern."

—"You bet. Goin' far?"

—"I guess not."

A common use of *you bet* is in response to *thank you* or *I appreciate it*. If you buy something in a Minnesota store—say a bag or two of tiny marshmallows for a salad—the sales clerk might say *thank you*, in which case you would say *you bet*. But generally the customer says *thank you* first in Minnesota, and the clerk says *you bet*.

You bet is mainly used to answer questions. If you can't think of anything else, say "You bet." *You bet* is meant to be pleasantly agreeable and doesn't obligate you to a strong position. In fact, hardly anything obligates you to a strong opinion in Minnesota.

—"Warm enough for you?"

—"You bet."

—"Walter Mondale's been keeping a pretty low profile since the election, hasn't he?"

—"You bet."

Sometimes the question is only implied.

—"I kinda like flannel pajamas."

—"You bet."

—"This humidity sorta gets to you."

—"You bet."

—"The heat I don't mind, it's the humidity."

—"You bet."

—"You get a real hot day, say 95 even, and with low humidity it's decent. But take a day when the humidity's about 100 percent and I don't care if the temperature's only 75, it's uncomfortable."

—"You bet."

It's worth pointing out that *you bet* has nothing to do with betting or gambling of any kind, even though Minnesota is the Bingo Capital of the Midwest. But *you bet* can occur in a Minnesota wagering situation, so don't be confused.

—"You want to go out to Bingo Bonanza after supper? There's a full moon, and today's date is half my age. It's my night."

—"You bet. I feel lucky, too. I'm gonna try playing twelve cards at once."

Pronunciation Note: Most Minnesotan phrases look like this: ——————— or this: ⟍
and sometimes this: ⟋⟍⟋⟍⟋⟍⟍
But this: ⟋⟍⟋⟋ or this: ⟋
would be big mistakes.

Minnesotan is not a musical language. Some people with an ax to grind have said it is the musical equivalent of a one-string guitar. What I say is, what's wrong with a monotone—at least you don't startle anybody, but it does mean that Minnesotans are not asked to be on talk shows as much as residents of other states, not that we care.

✓ *That's Different*

That's different is indispensable in Minnesota. *You bet* is a blanket reply on neutral ground, with the mere suggestion of opinion. *That's different* is deployed in all other cases, except where *whatever* is called for (see below). *That's different* means you have an opinion, but you're holding back the details. Here are two Minnesotans discussing bullhead bait.

—"I suppose you use night crawlers for bullheads?"

—"You bet. Whadda you use?"

—"Stink bait. I make it out of rotten hamburger and moldy cheese, with oatmeal for a binder."

—"That's different."

If somebody shows you the Holstein paneling he covered his living room walls with, you say

—"That's different."

If a new family moves in down the block and they've got four big dogs, six old cars, and three teenagers, you say

—"They're different."

If you are dining with Minnesotans during your visit and they ask you if you like the Macaroni/Herring/Pinto Bean hotdish staring up at you from your plate, you might say

—"You bet."

But probably you'd say

—"It's different."

✓ *Whatever*

Whatever expresses emotional turmoil of many varieties and takes over in Minnesota conversation when *you bet* and *that's different* won't do the job.

Whatever can be used to express disappointment.

—"Your work is good, Bud, we don't have any complaints, but we're gonna have to let you go. It's the economy."

—"Whatever."

Or it can express resignation.

—"I've been an electrician for twenty years, but I tell you this house of yours is the worst I've ever seen. I'm surprised you didn't have real trouble long before now. I'm gonna have to replace all the wiring. It ain't gonna be cheap."

—"Whatever."

If your wife tells you that her sister and brother-in-law are gonna come stay with you for a few months while they find themselves, you might say

—"You bet."

Or you might say

—"That's different."

But more than likely you'd say

—"Whatever."

Harold Mire Hosts the Gorbachevs

(Declassified Details Released in 1996)

After the fall of the Berlin Wall in 1989, Mikhail Gorbachev and his wife Raisa announced a stop in Minnesota on June 3, 1990, during their big tour of America. Most people I know out where I live on the southwestern Minnesota prairies, including my good friend and neighbor Harold Mire, figured it would turn out to be one of those typical deals where a bunch of Minnesota's Metro bigwigs would commandeer the festivities.

But miracles happen. Harold Mire's name was picked out of a hat by the Russian advance team in early May to represent all Minnesotans. Mikhail and Raisa Gorbachev would spend their six or so hours with Harold and his family in "Greater Minnesota," a term invented in the Twin Cities to sound better than "boondocks," which is how they really regarded rural Minnesota.

At the last minute, Governor Rudy Perpich was invited to ride along with the Harold and Gorby entourage, if he wanted to, in spite of the fact that his name was not drawn from the hat, but he declined.

Itinerary

1:00 P.M.—Mr. and Mrs. Gorbachev (R&MG) are greeted at MSP International by Harold Mire (HM), who has a clearance to drive his black 1980 LTD out on the tarmac. Harold tells Gorby through Boris, the translator and bodyguard, that it has 168,000 miles on it and counting. "It's got that great Ford V-8 in it." Gorby tells Harold he could get big bucks for that LTD back in Russia. Harold says it is not for sale.

1:05—Against his better judgment HM takes Crosstown west and holds it at seventy miles per hour, just below the threshold where it tends to shimmy. At the 35W infamous mixmaster interchange, where Crosstown narrows to one lane, Harold asks R&MG to join him in a moment of nondenominational prayer and gets his first good chuckle from the Gorbachevs.

1:12—HM drives through Burger King and orders two salads in those weird clear plastic greenhouse-style containers, with the dressing in little packets that tend to squirt every direction but toward the lettuce, as Boris finds out, to a car full of laughter, including his.

1:20—By request, Harold drives through Hardee's and orders a Big Beef for Gorby and a Fisherman's Fillet for Boris, who says nyet to the tartar sauce in the trick squirter.

1:30—Harold drives through McDonald's because Gorby wants to try his English. He says "Two large fries" into the drive-through menu board, but the girl at the pickup window gives him Chicken McNuggets. Raisa eats the McNuggets.

1:34—They eat in the car while heading southwesterly into Greater Minnesota on Highway 5, connecting to Highway 212 at Young America. Fast food leads to grogginess as R&MG take short snoozes. Boris shoots the bull with Harold about the Vikings.

2:50—Harold stops at an undisclosed self-service gas station. He fills the LTD with no-lead. The clerks watch from the window as two police cars pull up beside the LTD. Harold buys two twelve-ounce bottles of water at the C-store for eighty cents each. MG says, "Eighty cents for a cup of water? That's more expensive than the gas per gallon." Harold says, "It's a rip-off, Gorby, but people have been conditioned to think tap water and well water are no good. It's called marketing." MG slaps his knee and laughs at that capitalism joke.

3:35—Harold drives by an old and defunct coal-fired generating plant where a power company wants to burn PCB-contaminated oils contrary to the wishes of area citizens. MG is reminded of the darker days under Stalin.

3:52—They arrive at Harold's place in the country, south of Hanley Falls and north of Cottonwood, where R&MG are greeted by HM's wife, Ethel. Daughter Lily says "Howdy" and then leaves for her church-league softball game, an important grudge match between Holy Redeemer and Our Savior's. Raisa wonders out loud if it is common for American churches to battle with each other on the playing fields. Harold is about to reply to Raisa, but Ethel reads him like a book and taps his shoulder.

What the Gorbachevs and the Mires did in the next two hours is pretty much undisclosed, but Harold surely mentioned the recent good rains making the prairies come alive. Gorby and Harold without a doubt also looked at Harold's brother's corn crop, a good nine inches high by then. The soybeans were just peeping through the topsoil.

For their part, Ethel and Raisa took a walk on the gravel road that runs east and west past the Mire place so they could talk privately.

The biggest show Harold and Ethel provided had to be the native flowers and the birds, the best in twenty years, Harold told the Gorbachevs. At the Mire place so far that spring they had seen a cardinal, an American redstart, three goldfinches, Baltimore orioles, mourning doves, crows, downy woodpeckers, wrens, and the day before their visit, a nesting pair of indigo buntings.

5:45—With a sack of Ethel's health-nut oatmeal cookies to control munchies on the trip back to Minneapolis, the Gorbachevs depart Ryan Field in Marshall in a rented Piper Aztec, with Raisa and Ethel in the backseat, Harold as pilot, and Gorby in the right seat. They see the sweep of the rich farming country and small towns from 5500 feet, flying through the cleanest air in the nation. Harold lets Gorby take the controls for a few minutes. Gorby says, "You didn't hear me say it, but I could get used to this life." "You bet," says Harold, "a guy couldn't do better."

6:05—In the Twin Cities area, on approach to Minneapolis International, R&MG look down on the future site of the Mall of America, Canterbury Downs, and the Humphrey Dome. After landing, Harold taxis the Aztec behind the Follow Me truck to the Russian equivalent of Air Force One.

Ethel and Raisa hug each other, and contrary to everything Gorby had heard about Minnesota men, Harold gives him a bear hug, which raises a big cheer from the Minnesotans behind the security fences.

Lesson 2

The Power of the Negative

 ## A Word About Emotional Outbursts

—"Oh, great, just wonderful, terrific. I love it!!!"

Get that excited about something in Minnesota and you might as well paste a bumper sticker on your forehead that says I'M NOT FROM AROUND HERE. I don't know what you were taught where you came from, but you shouldn't let your positive feelings run amuck while you're here. It's okay to have good feelings but there's no sense running down the street telling people about it at the top of your voice. There's a good chance it won't last, anyway. Good things happen—yes—but when they do, Minnesotans are a little nervous because they know something bad will eventually happen to balance it out. But if something bad happens they know they're safe for a while from something else bad, probably, but you never know.

If you have to overdo it in Minnesota, overdo it on the downside, not the upside.

Minnesotans prefer to express their positive feelings through the use of negatives, because it naturally levels things out. This will be one of your hardest lessons, and don't expect to learn it overnight. Some people who were born in Minnesota still haven't got the hang of it.

If you just got married or bought a late-model pickup under book price with low mileage and hardly any rust, or it's dawn on opening day of the duck season, a Minnesotan would say

—"I wouldn't want you to think I'm not happy."

That's a strong statement here.

Phrases

✓ *It could be worse*

✓ *Not too bad*

✓ *Not so bad*

✓ *Can't complain*

If somebody asks "How's it goin'?" and you're feeling mainly average and life in general is okay at the moment—not perfect, of course—you'll say

—"Not so bad."

On the other hand, if you're feeling better than average and you haven't noticed any ill winds, you'll say

—"Can't complain."

Can't complain actually means you could complain if pressed, because there's always something, that's just the way it is. But you're saying that since you feel so good (within reason) for the moment—with no illusions that it's permanent or anything—you're going to pass on the complaining for now, but you'll catch up on it later.

If you reply

—"It could be worse,"

you could be saying exactly what you mean, because of course things can always be worse than they are. In fact, things can be worse than they are more often than they can be better than they are; it's a fact of life. If it's not going real well—say the pipes busted in the basement while you were in town seeing the sheriff about your stolen car—you say "It could be worse" because you know very well that if you start thinking this is the end of it, the water heater's gonna short out or your daughter's gonna need braces.

TV reporters hired from other states generally come out of the chutes too fast and aren't properly trained for Minnesota-style reporting. So when the Action News Team takes the helicopter out to the site of a tornado touchdown, these newcomers generally end up putting a microphone in a Minnesotan's face and asking how he feels. I know that goes over on the coasts, but in Minnesota we'll just look at you over the tops of our glasses.

Picture a farmer standing in what's left of his farmyard. A tornado has leveled all his buildings. The family went to the cellar when they saw frequent lightning flashes and heard the freight train rolling through miles from the nearest track—but when they came out all they saw was horizon with tree stumps, a tractor on top of the old corncrib, and several soft objects like straw and typewriter paper stuck into hard objects like trees. The camera takes a good look at total destruction—you can hear the news anchors back at the station clucking—and then closes in on the farmer's face. The reporter says:

—"How do you feel?"

—"It could be worse. I think we can salvage some of the lumber from the barn. That pile over there looks pretty good. It'll be a smaller barn—some of the boards are in the next county."

Tears begin to well up in the reporter's eyes.

—"It must be terrible for you, the mixture of emotions, the shock."

—"Well, not really. It happens, you know. It's not like we didn't expect it."

The reporter begins weeping. The producer cuts to the news anchors back in the Twin Cities. They are holding each other, weeping. The reporter is barely able to squeeze out the next question:

—"Where do you go from here? I'm sorry for breaking up like this—it's so awful."

—"We're not going anyplace. I'm gonna set up the tent over there where the granary used to be and then work on getting the top story back on the house. Look at that thing, would you?"

—"John, Nina—back to you. I can't take it anymore."

When John and Nina get the reins, they turn to the weatherman at their left and say in unison:

—"Well, Larry, can you explain this for us?"

Suddenly all over Minnesota we're listening again. It's the weather. We believe in the weather here. It's something to hang on to. And we believe in our TV weather people. Larry goes right into the twenty-four-hour satellite loop that shows the buildup of the clouds that produced the tornado. His voice is controlled when he talks about the warm front from the Gulf and the cold front from Canada, and the humidity. We get all the facts. In Minnesota the 10 o'clock news is just the window dressing for the 10 o'clock weather. The low-keyed attempt to explain something out of our control puts us right in the mood for a good night's sleep.

For practice with the Minnesota negatives, try translating these foreign statements into Minnesotan:

1. *I'm so happy, I can't believe it!!*

2. *That's the best movie I've seen in twenty years!!*

3. *Oh, darling, this is our twentieth anniversary!!!!*

Answers:

1. *Yeah, well, boy!*

2. *It sure beats some of that other stuff they've been charging us seven bucks to watch.*

3. *Twenty years—not too bad a deal, huh? Pass the butter, please.*

One last note: *not too good* and *not so good* are worse than *not too bad* and *not so bad*. Way worse, in fact. When somebody asks you how you slept on the guest bed with the bar that cuts across your back and gives you shooting pains down your legs, you will say "Not too bad" because you don't want to hurt their feelings, but how you actually slept was *not too good*.

All-in-One
Prom Kit

The ALL-IN-ONE PROM KIT has everything you and your date will need for a successful prom, packaged in a handsome cardboard box with your class motto printed on the side. Each PROM KIT contains a carnation, a corsage, a formal, and a tux—with all the extras: aftershave, perfume, clean hankies, simulated pearl necklace, socks, and shoes.

Thousands of PROM KITS have been sold at $99.99, but now, while supplies last, you can purchase the ALL-IN-ONE PROM KIT for the incredible price of $19.95.

The music will stop and the dancers will stare when you and your date enter the gymnasium wearing your ALL-IN-ONE PROM KIT.

Please specify pink or green formal
with or without shoulder straps.
One size should fit all
if you work at it.

ABOUT THE ADVERTISEMENTS IN THIS GUIDE

If I had known what this book was going to cost me (but you hardly ever know anything, really, until it's too late), I would never have put the first word on the page, or been so foolishly happy about it back when it was just a feeble idea in my weak brain. Normally, I'm the kind of guy that likes to sit around looking out at whatever comes his way. It can be dull, yes, but what else is new?

When I started this book I was short on cash, but that was inconsequential, because I couldn't think of anything I needed. But that changed pretty fast. When push came to shove, I thought about putting a mortgage on the farmhouse to take care of loose ends while I plugged along on the book, but the bank said they didn't think the house would last long enough for me to pay off the loan. They said my house was depreciating at about 10 percent a year and that in ten years it would be worth nothing in the housing market. They told me to bulldoze the house and move into an apartment. So then I asked the loan officer if I could use the book I hadn't written yet as collateral. That cracked him up. He got all the bank employees together and had me repeat what I said. It made their day.

I took my hat in hand and tried to get some financial backing from the larger Minnesota companies whose names are household words, but they said they didn't feel they wanted their name in a book with as little chance of success as this one. So I went to smaller Minnesota businesses and the result is plain. The Chicken-Feather Siding Company, Bob Humde Enterprises, Walleye Phone, and all the rest were willing to toss a couple of bucks my way for the commercial exposure. I hope I don't sound like I don't appreciate it.

I have printed their ads exactly as they sent them to me. I apologize if you find some of the ads a little low on the totem pole of taste, but it's the best I could do and the best they could do. These ads weren't dreamed up by fancy ad agencies.

I wish I could give you my personal guarantee that the products and services advertised in this book are what they seem to be, but I can't, because I haven't tried everything. But

Baxter Bus Tours Of Minnesota

CARNIVAL OF CRAZY DAYS: A non-stop, twenty-four-hour whirlwind bus tour of Crazy Days in ten different Minnesota towns. Complimentary Minnesota breakfast, complimentary Minnesota nap about two in the afternoon—we'll park the bus in the shade for you. Plenty of cargo space for your bargains. The tour concludes with MIDNITE MADNESS.

And if you're interested in our educational system, Baxter's SUMMER SCHOOLHOUSE Tour could be just the ticket for you. It's a seven-day package, with transportation by certified school bus—no smoking, no yelling, stay in your seats while in motion. Visit up to four school buildings per day in selected towns. Each stop includes a guided tour by the superintendent, sack lunch and a couple pans of bars in the cafeteria, a brief program of choral music and humorous readings, and observation of floor waxing by janitors. Bring your tennis shoes—we always give you time to shoot a few baskets in the gym. Sock feet okay, but not responsible for accidents.

TOURS $ 5.75 PER DAY FOR

BAXTER BUS TOURS—simple, down-to-earth vacations on a bus with people like yourself. It's the next best thing to never leaving home.

still, I kind of hope that you'll do your best to patronize my advertisers. They took a chance with me, so keep that in mind as you thumb through it in the bookstore.

A couple of the companies are the subjects of class-action suits at present, but it is not my place to mention which ones—they're innocent until proven guilty in my book. If you're upset with one of my advertisers, please, don't contact me—just write a letter to the Minnesota Pretty Good Business Bureau. That's their job and they're not too bad at it, in a way, I guess.

And if you buy the book and wish you hadn't, I'm sorry—it's the best I could do. If it's not good enough, well, what can I say. I really did try. But I've had failures before, so don't worry about me. I'll be okay.

FISCAL ADJUSTMENTS TO LESSONS AND ADS

It is my obligation to mention that because of the rise in the cost of living over the past twenty-five years, any mention of the cost of a product or service should be multiplied by 4, with food items having a multiplier of 5.5. Prescription drug prices from 1987 should be multiplied by 10.

For example, in the advertisement for the ALL-IN-ONE PROM KIT on page 13, the bargain price listed at $19.95 would be $79.80 as of the last day of 2011.

The company manufacturing the fashion kit declared bankruptcy soon after the *Minneapolis Star Tribune* in May of 1996 printed the headline PROM NIGHT WARDROBE MALFUNCTION, the very first use of the term, long before any Super Bowl shenanigans. The charming couple wearing their ALL-IN-ONE kits were the hit of the prom as they rushed off the dance floor in absolutely total scantily clad misery and embarrassment. But times change and that same couple kept up their friendship. By 2010 they were living together in an apartment in the University of Minnesota's Dinkytown and thought it would be a hoot to upload their malfunctions to YouTube from old video cam footage taken by the principal. They were pulling in 1,458 views a day for three days of glory. They were friended a lot on Facebook, but wardrobe malfunctions were a dime a dozen way back in 2010. In 2011 several high schools specifically forbid the execution of "wardrobe malfunctions" at the prom, or for that matter, in the halls and classrooms. There was a story going around Facebook that certain high fashion women's clothing had built-in "wardrobe malfunction release levers." No surprise that it was a Facebook "fact malfunction." No such device existed. Then.

BAXTER'S BUS TOURS ad on page 15 had the incredible price of $5.75 per day, with sack lunch. What fun it was to motor around at low speed and see those old brick school buildings. The odors and fragrances alone brought back many memories of one's elementary school days. Most of those buildings have now been bulldozed or declared unsafe. But ol' Baxter is still at it. The tours today don't create much of the overwhelming nostalgia that was the heart of the tours in the 1980s. What with the high price of gas, one of the biggest stories of the last twenty-five years, Baxter now charges well over ten times the old 1987 price. This slow but rather exciting tour of summer schoolhouses now will set you back $135.99 a day per person, including the cost of a FEDERALLY mandated FBI background check.

Eating In in Minnesota

 **HOTDISH**

On your visit to Minnesota, you will sooner or later come face-to-face with Minnesota's most popular native food, *hotdish*. It can grace any table. A traditional main course, *hotdish* is cooked and served hot in a single baking dish and commonly appears at family reunions and church suppers. *Hotdish* is constructed on a base of canned cream of mushroom soup and canned vegetables. The other ingredients are as varied as the Minnesota landscape. If you sit down to something that doesn't look like anything you've ever seen before, it's probably *hotdish*.

As of the November 1986 state hotdish survey, there were 3,732 different hotdish recipes in Minnesota, up twelve from the previous November. Here are eight hotdishes taken at random from that survey.

Spaghetti-Tuna Hotdish

Garbanzo Bango Hotdish

Velveeta-Hamburger Hotdish

Ketchup Surprise Hotdish

Back of the Refrigerator Hotdish

Doggone Good Hotdish

Turkey Wiener Doodah Hotdish (1985 Winner of Le Grande Prix de Hotdish)

Organ Meat–Cashew Hotdish

If you're visiting Minnesota in late August, the Hotdish Pavilion at the Minnesota State Fair is quite the deal. You have to see it to believe it. You'll get your fill of hotdish and hotdish-style entertainment.

The three-volume *Official State Hotdish Cookbook* can be ordered from the Hotdish Institute, Mendota Heights. Major credit cards accepted. If you order before the end of 1987, you will also receive the beautiful album (cassette or eight-track) of the most loved hotdish songs, with baritone Ernie "Hotdish" Johnson and his Mushroom Band. Order before Memorial Day and you will also receive *Hotdish on the Prairie*, a collection of poems by Minnesota's best-known food poets.

If you want to try experimenting at home with hotdish before your visit, here's a generic recipe. Roughly speaking, anything goes.

GENERIC HOTDISH (FOR 4)

Mix together in a large bowl:

2 cans cream of mushroom soup
1 pound cooked pulverized meat
2 cans of vegetables.

Stir.

Salt to taste.

Pour into baking dish.

Sprinkle with canned french-fried onion rings or Chow Mein noodles.

Bake at 400 degrees until a brown crust forms.

Howard Mohr

HOTDISH: AN UPDATE

"Eating In in Minnesota" needs only one or two minor tweaks after twenty-five years. So dive in. You have nothing to fear but fear itself if you use any of the original dialogues as you learn Minnesota-style dining, munching, and mealtime socializing. Your hosts will love you for trying.

The Hotdish Institute of Mendota Heights says that hotdish is still number one on the Minnesota Food Pyramid, and no competitors are even close. Hotdish has also retained its status as the Official State Food. In 1986 there were 3,732 different hotdish recipes extant. On the last day of 2011 there were 4,123 documented hotdish recipes, a significant increase. The random list of hotdishes in Lesson 3 is pretty much accurate up through "Doggone Good Hotdish."

But a bit of a black eye for the Hotdish Institute is the "Turkey Weiner Doodah Hotdish," which was awarded the 1985 winner of Le Grand Prix de Hotdish by France. An intensive investigation conducted by a graduate student in culinology at the U of M in 1993 turned up solid evidence that this sick joke was perpetrated by two French chefs. The Hotdish Institute sought and received an apology from the Honorary Consul General of France in St. Paul, Minnesota, but that heartless prank continues to leave a bad taste in the mouths of hotdish aficionados statewide.

I am sad to say that there is no longer a Hotdish Pavilion at the Minnesota State Fair. It was destroyed by fire in 2003. According to the fire marshal, the flames seemed to originate very near where the institute president was attempting to use a propane torch to light the pool of brandy in the center of the ten-foot-diameter Hotdish Flambé, a new recipe created by the Hotdish Institute for a fund-raiser. There were no injuries except to the reputation of the institute.

The Generic Hotdish recipe is still valid and is a good starter recipe for newcomers to Minnesota. In 1997 the institute added one additional baking tip received from a time-strapped working mother who needed to get the hotdish on the table fast. Instead of waiting around for it to bake at four

21 |

hundred degrees until a brown crust formed, she just turned the oven to CLEAN.

BARBECUES

The barbecue is a Minnesota sandwich consisting of boiled ketchup and hamburger served on a white buttered bun. It is commonly eaten with a spoon.

—"Hand me another napkin, please. This *barbecue* is not too bad, but it's running down my arm."

The barbecue should not be confused with the Minnesota *taco*, pronounced *tack-oh*. The Minnesota *taco* consists of ketchup and hamburger served inside a folded tortilla (pronounced *tore-till-a*) and topped with Cheese Whiz. Many cooks substitute pickled herring for the hamburger and use cream of mushroom soup instead of Cheese Whiz as a topping. Lettuce is optional. Buttered and folded white bread can be substituted for the tortillas. It is commonly eaten with a spoon.

—"Hand me another napkin, please. This *taco* is not too bad, but it's running down my arm. It sort of reminds me of the *barbecues* we had yesterday."

THE MINNESOTA SALAD

The Minnesota Salad is an appetizing complement to any hotdish and is composed of Jell-O in any flavor, miniature colored marshmallows, canned fruit cocktail, and a generous dollop of Cool Whip on top. A common variant is to mix the Cool Whip with the Jell-O and sprinkle the marshmallows on top and omit the fruit.

—"Boy, pass me some more of that salad. I love marshmallows with my pork chops."

Don't make the mistake of calling the Minnesota salad *dessert* or saving it until the end of the meal.

The Minnesota tossed salad consists of a few leaves of iceberg lettuce floating on a sea of french dressing. It is acceptable to drink the dressing when you finish the lettuce.

 # THE THREE SQUARES

Breakfast

Breakfast occurs in the morning and is very close to the national standard. You get up and sit in your bathrobe and stare until the coffee is done. Maybe you have a doughnut with your second cup. When the other members of your household wander in, you don't speak unless spoken to. Your radio is on. The announcers themselves got up early in the morning and had a cup of coffee before they drove to the station in their bathrobes. They sound happy, but it is a dog's life, getting paid to sound happy in the morning.

Dinner

The Minnesota *dinner* is served at 12 noon sharp and is the major meal of the day. In smaller towns the fire whistle goes off right on the money so everybody can stop at once.

Supper

The Minnesota *supper* is served after 5 but before the 6 o'clock news on TV—which is announced with another blast on the fire whistle—and typically consists of leftovers from dinner, although many people fry up a few potatoes for extra bulk in the winter.

Lunch and a Little Lunch

In Minnesota, lunch is typically eaten three times a day. Lunch is situated before, after, and between breakfast, dinner, and supper. The mid-afternoon lunch occurs between 3 and 3:30. The morning lunch occurs at 10, or shortly thereafter.

If a Minnesotan says:

—"Do you want lunch?"

Your reply should not be:

—"Lunch? In the middle of the morning? I think I'll just wait till noon like an ordinary human being."

Lunch commonly consists of a drink—coffee, punch, or Kool-Aid—and a large tray of meat sandwiches on snack buns, fresh-baked cinnamon rolls, and several varieties of the native dessert called *bars*.

—"Oh, boy, *lunch*, it's been over two hours since *dinner* and I'm real hungry again."

A Little Lunch

Lunch can also occur at other odd times of the day. It is then called "a little lunch."

—"Well, what do you say, shall we have a little lunch?"

Little has no more to do with size and variety in the phrase "a little lunch" than it does when you say "I had a little trouble" after the parking brake fails on your car and it rolls through the wall into the No Smoking section of the Perkins Family Restaurant.

Wherever two or three are gathered together, a little lunch will be forthcoming: at 4-H, poker games, Lutheran Circle, piano recitals, town council, funerals, weddings. The little lunch is always larger than the mid-morning and mid-afternoon lunch, with a better selection of bars and meat sandwiches. You can easily make a meal out of it.

 ## A WORD ABOUT GRADUATION NIGHT IN MINNESOTA

On the night the local high school has graduation, the parents of the graduates each put on a little lunch. This is the biggest little lunch of the year. If you've lived in the same area most of your life, then you could be invited to as many as twenty graduation lunches. We call it the "night of the long lunch." You are expected to drive around to every lunch site and not only put in an appearance, but load up your plate with mints, ham sandwiches on snack buns, bars, and potato salad. Wear loose clothing as you begin the journey, or you might need professional help undressing when you get home after midnight.

Several times during your visit with Minnesotans you will be asked if you want a little lunch. In Minnesota a person is never left sitting without a plate of food for long. The good host will offer food every two hours and keep it in plain view between offers. Never refuse lunch when it is offered, although you can request smaller portions without penalty.

 ## ACCEPTING FOOD ON THE THIRD OFFER

Abrupt and eager acceptance of any offer is a common mistake made by Minnesota's visitors. If a Minnesotan says:

—"Can I get you a cup of coffee?"

You should not say:

—"Yeah, that would be great, thanks, with a little cream and sugar. And how about one of those cookies?"

We never accept until the third offer and then reluctantly. On the other hand, if a Minnesotan does not make an offer three times, it is not serious. Besides, those aren't cookies on the tray, they're bars, as you can see from their rectangular shape and the thickness of the Rice Krispie center.

Basic Phrases

✓ *I really couldn't.*
✓ *I can't let you.*
✓ *I shouldn't.*

Dialogue

—"Want a cup of coffee before you go?"

—"No, I wouldn't want to put you out. I'll get by."

—"You sure? Just made a fresh pot."

—"You didn't have to go and do that."

—"How about it, one cup?"

—"Well, if it's going to hurt your feelings, but don't fill it full."

—"How about a bar with that?"

—"I appreciate it, but no, really, I shouldn't."

—"They're Double Crispie Foghorn Bars."

—"I can't. I got my mind made up. I'm not gonna let you give me one."

—"There's one already cut with your name on it."

—"Whatever."

—"Cream for that coffee?"

—"No, no, no. That's okay, I can drink it black."

—"No problem. I'll get you some cream."

—"No, stay put. I don't need it."

—"You sure? It's just right out there in the refrigerator."

—"Well, if you're going that way anyway. I don't want you to make a special trip."

—"Sugar?"

—"I don't have to have sugar in my coffee . . ."

(Continue the above dialogue, adding other food items for practice.)

Special Note: In some non-food situations, Minnesota offers and refusals can be speeded up, as, for example, if you have lost your footing while removing snow from the roof of your house and are hanging by your feet from the rain gutter. Use your best judgment.

—"Want some help?"

—"No, that's okay, I've got one foot worked loose."

—"No problem. I'm right here."

—"I got into this, I'll get out of it."

—"You look uncomfortable."

—"Well, maybe you could hold my shoulders while I twist around."

 DESSERT NEGOTIATION

In this lesson you learn how to get all the dessert you want and deserve without appearing to want or desire it. That's the way we do it: It's okay to want something, we just don't believe in showing it.

Phrases

✓ *Just a sliver.*
✓ *About half that.*
✓ *If you insist.*
✓ *I'm trying to cut down.*
✓ *Boogie Beat Bongo Bar?*

Dialogue

(Two Minnesotans at the Sunday dinner dessert table. The hostess speaks first.) Here's your motivation: When you line up for Minnesota dessert, you are only helping out the people who went to all the trouble to make that sea of sweets. If you don't eat their desserts, it's like a slap in the face. So even if you don't want dessert, you should take some, or suffer the consequences. There is little difference between refusing dessert in order to get all you want and refusing dessert because you don't want any. It comes to the same thing: a plateful of dessert.

HOSTESS: "How about some pie?"

GUEST: "I don't need it, really, I'm sort of on a diet, but maybe just a sliver of the coconut creme."

H: "How about the Dutch apple?"

G: "Well, I shouldn't, but go ahead. Just a taste, though, and leave off the ice cream."

H: "It's homemade. Ralph cranked it up this morning."

G: "Homemade ice cream. It'd be a crime to pass that up, wouldn't it?"

H: "Silver Doodle Velvet sheet cake? I know Darlene brought it especially for you."

G: "About half of what you gave Bill there. I'm trying to cut down."

H: "There's one Roll Me Over caramel nougat bar left. Why don't you eat it? Go ahead. Then we can wash the pan."

G: "It's the least I can do, I guess. But then I'm gonna have to go lie down awhile."

H: "Can you get it all on that plate?"

G: "No problem, I can stack up a couple of things and pile it in the middle there."

☞ SUNDAY DINNER

Some Minnesotans insist that Sunday dinner start at 12 noon sharp like the other six dinners of the week, but the standard is closer to 1 P.M., and can be as late as 1:30 if the sermon was long or if the oven did not go on automatically at 9:30 while you were deep in the examination of the first chapter of Romans in Sunday school.

If you are invited to Sunday dinner in Minnesota, don't make plans for later in the day. After you eat you are obligated to move into the living room for conversation conducted through yawns. If there's no football game on TV or you can't hold your eyes open any longer or you are listing in the lounger more than forty-five degrees, you should go someplace where you can lose consciousness without drawing attention to yourself with unusual body noises.

—"After a meal like that a guy gets logy."

—"Why don't you take that back bedroom. There's a comforter in the closet behind the card table."

By 3:45, everybody will be strung around the house sawing logs. Don't just lie down and read magazines or snoop in the drawers. Take off your shoes and go to sleep. You should have crease marks on your face from the bedspread when you come back out around 5:30 or 6.

Many Minnesotans feel more comfortable napping on top of their own beds. They excuse themselves and drive home—if it's less than twenty miles—for a snooze. But when it's time to haul out the leftovers at the meal site, they drive back and complete their Sunday obligation.

Out of bed, dress for church, Sunday dinner, nap, leftover supper, coffee and bars, and back in bed. It's a complete Sunday package. Bailing out at any point would be a mistake without a legitimate reason or two.

—"Johnnie's throwing up. We better head out."

—"The headlights bit the dust on the way down. We gotta get home before dark. I think it's a short."

—"I'm not sure I shut the gate on the cattle yard."

When you leave early, you will be given a bag of leftovers. Don't refuse it.

Slow-Decay Snack Cakes:
A Disclaimer

I regret to say that SLOW-DECAY SNACK CAKES, our most generous and popular sponsor of *How to Talk Minnesotan*, can no longer be sold in stores—a crime really, after years of being voted the best food item for the winter survival kits that all Minnesotans keep in the trunks of their cars in case they are snowbound for a day or two. I also regret that I was compelled to place the following announcement from Borderline Drugs, LLC, as per its takeover of the Slow-Decay company.

In 2009 our lab experts at Borderline, ever vigilant to find expensive drugs, discovered by chance that aceto-porxo-myo-cina-razza-trin, the main ingredient in SLOW-DECAY SNACK CAKES, had incredible medicinal properties. Aceto-porxo-myo-cina-razza-trin is now sold only by prescription as RAZZATRIN™. It is a red capsule with black dots and a single yellow band that glows in the dark. Just ask your doctor if the "red pill with black dots and a single yellow band that glows in the dark" is right for you.

Do not continue to take RAZZATRIN if you experience mild blindness, increased blood pressure, or begin seeing things that others can't see, such as snakes or UFOs. In some cases RAZZATRIN, instead of lowering your cholesterol, can increase it, but that is very rare, and we believe it is a fairly good bet this will not happen to you, but if it does, well, nothing ventured, nothing gained, and we feel for you.

Dizziness, vertigo, hair loss, and constipation will very likely occur, along with a few rather personal side effects we would rather not mention.

Lesson 4

Basic Conversations

CARRYING THE BALL

The basic Minnesota conversation consists of a statement or a question, followed by a reply.

—"Been havin' pretty good luck with that Ford?"

—"You bet."

Again:

—"Shall we have warmed-up hotdish for breakfast?"

—"It's okay by me. You only go around once."

Again:

—"Ol' Daryl caught a walleye trolling with a Daredevil."

—"That was dumb luck."

A longer conversation would be multiples of this basic unit.

If you are called upon to start a conversation from a dead stop in Minnesota you should know that 35 percent of our conversations deal with the weather, 30 percent with cars, 15 percent with food, 10 percent with road and building construction, 9 percent with fishing, 1 percent with politics and religion, and 1 percent with the rest.

If you get into a tight spot, pick a subject, form it into a statement or question, and you'll be right in the middle of a lively exchange. In the following conversation, four popular subjects have been skillfully intertwined.

—"I see they're talkin' about thunderstorms tomorrow."

—"You bet. And I just washed my car."

—"Good for fishin' though, huh?"

—"You can say that again. But it's gonna make it pretty muddy for the crew putting in that bypass out there on County 12."

—"The thing is, do we really need it? We've been bypassed enough in this town."

A Word About the Minnesota Language System Phrase Cap

(Copyright 1986, patent pending)

You can increase your chances of having a nice visit in Minnesota by buying yourself a Minnesota Language Systems Phrase Cap to complement this guidebook. The Minnesota Phrase Cap features the name of a seed corn company, or a tractor, or a herbicide of your choice emblazoned above the bill. If you don't specify in your order, you will receive either a green John Deere or a green Pioneer phrase cap. One size fits all, mostly, unless you have an unusually big head or a lot of hair, or your ears are too high. In that case, order the jumbo.

Inside the phrase cap you'll find a hundred handy Minnesota phrases that will get you out of almost any conversational jam. Whenever a Minnesotan speaks to you, remove your cap, run your hand through your hair with your free hand, and then look inside the phrase cap for your reply. Looking inside a cap during a conversation is a perfectly natural act here.

Don't let the pause disturb you as you search for your answer. Long silences are the heartbeat of a Minnesota conversation. A quick answer is a sure sign that you're not from around here or you're hiding something.

—"How's life treatin' you?"

—[*Look in cap*] "Not so bad. Can't complain. It could be worse."

Feed caps can be worn anywhere, anytime. [With some exceptions: See *Feed* elsewhere in this guide for more fashion information on feed caps.]

☞ WEATHER CONVERSATIONS

If you can't carry on a conversation about the weather in Minnesota, you might as well pack your bags and head back to where you came from. One day the clerk at the Red Owl said to this guy ahead of me in line, "What d'ya think of this weather?" And this guy's face got red and he said

—"I don't think anything. I don't pay any attention. What weather? Are you kidding me? Do I know you?"

That was not a good reply for Minnesota.

Here are two Minnesotans getting wound up on the weather.

—"What d'ya think of this weather?"

—"Boy, it's something."

—"I've never seen anything like it."

—"You got that right."

In specific weather conditions the conversation becomes more detailed and animated. For example, in the fog.

—"It's foggy, isn't it?"

—"You talk about fog, this is it."

—"I wonder what causes a fog like this?"

—"That's an interesting question. They say it's the cold ground meeting the warm moist air. But don't quote me."

—"It makes a guy wonder."

Many weather conversations deal with predictions.

—"It's gonna do something."

—"Yeah, I don't like the looks of those clouds."

—"The birds are acting funny."

—"And the air."

—"Feels kinda thick or something."

—"I'd say it could do anything."

—"A guy wants to keep his eye on weather like this."

A warm day with no wind and plenty of sun will be your toughest lesson. It's not for beginners, but then it doesn't come up all that much either.

—"Pretty nice day then, huh?"

—"It could be worse, but it won't last. You get a day like this, it spells trouble. It's too good."

—"I know what you mean."

—"It makes a guy nervous."

—"Uneasy."

—"You got that right."

MINNESOTA WEATHER TALK: AN UPDATE

The kind of casual weather talk a guy would exchange with his neighbor if he met him on the street or at the post office has not changed much.

"So what do you think of this weather then?" works just fine as an opener, since it does not point to any radical opinion the speaker might have or trample on any weather beliefs held dear by the listener.

Your reply should be: "It's something isn't it? They say it's gonna rain, but what do they know?" This reply sounds slightly opinionated, but what keeps it in the civil range of casual weather talk is the use of "they," an unnamed entity whose role is to accept blame: "they" are traditionally wrong, whoever they are, so nobody gets upset.

Weather has always been a pretty safe topic for conversation in Minnesota, as topics go, certainly safer than "How about them Vikings?" This question would lead right into opinions on the draft, the quarterback, and the coach. That sort of talk can heat up fast.

Weather talk is still safe in 2012, but I would be remiss doing this update of the original *How to Talk Minnesotan* if I did not mention something new that has emerged in Minnesota weather. One should tread carefully in any discussions of this wind debate.

Straight-Line Winds versus Tornadoes

The following dialogue took place the morning after what the media said had been a destructive straight-line wind in southern Minnesota. Ned and Kyle, both farmers, met at the gas pumps in town, filling up their pickups with four-dollar-a-gallon diesel.

NED: "Say, Kyle, did you lose any trees in that straight-line wind we had yesterday?"

KYLE: "They say it got up to 120 miles per hour, and I believe it, but in my opinion it was not a straight line per se.* I lost a spruce and there's no doubt it was twisted right out of the ground, and only a tornado could do that kind of damage."

NED: "Yahbut, was there a funnel? You gotta have a funnel, Kyle."

KYLE: "Well, it was not a visible twister but it felt like a twister is how I'd put it, what with things going every which way. I don't know what else you'd call it."

NED: "I don't wanna get on your bad side this early in the morning, Kyle, but my machine shed was pushed downwind for almost a quarter mile as the crow flies, and not a twist anywhere on it, Kyle. It broke off all the support poles and left the sheet metal in a neat pile, worthless of course, except for recycling it to the junkyard. Steel prices are up, so it will be off to China with the shed is my guess."

KYLE: "You are welcome to your opinion about the wind, Ned. But what about your tractor? Didn't you have your biggest tractor in there?"

NED: "Well, it was sitting in the shed facing south, but now it's out in the open facing north. I suppose you're gonna tell me it was hit by a twister that whirled it one hundred eighty degrees?"

KYLE: "I wouldn't try to tell you anything, but it seems pretty obvious."

NED: "Whatever."**

* Use of "per se" in Minnesotan is rare, but it has started to show up in weather talk especially, though I have to admit that it sticks out like a sore thumb, and I would not recommend its habitual use in Minnesota.

** Ned has used "whatever" since "whatever" can be construed by the listener any way he wants it, and Kyle's "You can say that again" defuses the discussion.

KYLE: "You can say that again."

NED: "What do you say we go over to the Legion Hall and eat some of those sweet rolls that look like horse turds with frosting."

KYLE: "Sounds good to me."

As the result of the controversy over straight-line winds versus tornadoes, an obscure rural Minnesota poet has blossomed into celebrity with his instructive poem that definitively explains how to recognize the imminent arrival of a tornado and, more importantly, clearly allows folks to determine if it was indeed a tornado that went through, thereby ruling out straight-line winds.

How to Tell a Tornado

Listen for noises.
If you do not live
near railroad tracks,
the freight train you hear
is not the Northern Pacific
lost in the storm:
that is a tornado
doing imitations of itself.
One of its favorite sounds
is no sound.
After the high wind,
and before the freight train,
there is a pocket of nothing:
this is when you think
everything has stopped:
but do not be fooled.
Leave it all behind
except for a candle
and take to the cellar.

Afterwards
if straws are imbedded

in trees without leaves,
and your house—except
for the unbroken bathroom mirror—
has vanished without a trace,
and you are naked
except for the right leg of your pants,
you can safely assume
that a tornado
has gone through your life
without touching it.

MINNESOTA TWEETS

Twitter is nothing new to Minnesotans. As you can see from the exchanges in Lesson 4, a basic conversational give-and-take can be conducted with way fewer characters than the 140 allowed in contemporary Tweets. In Minnesotan we go one step further, restricting basic conversational exchanges to thirty syllables.

Here's a friendly exchange that was conducted with a total of eleven syllables:

—"Having pretty good luck with that Ford?"

—"You bet."

Here's a lively morning exchange completed successfully with twenty-two syllables:

—"Shall we have warmed-up hotdish for breakfast?"

—"It's okay by me. You only go around once."

Neither of these exchanges comes close to using 140 characters.

The topics of basic conversation in Minnesota have not changed much in twenty-five years.

What makes Minnesota Twitter so popular, even with some teenagers, is that it is conducted in everyday conversations, and no texting is required, no computer is required; in fact, all that is required is people having conversations as always, with pretty good give-and-takes, and way fewer than 140 characters. The only "characters" in Minnesota Twitter are the people themselves.

Newcomers to Minnesota need to know that talking weather is a primary skill. Practice the exchanges in "Weather Conversations" and you will soon accomplish three things: You will be on the road to fluency, you will be doing it in Minnesota Twitter, and you will be making friends besides.

Minnesotans can meet and tweet about the weather or the chances of the Vikings making it to the Super Bowl this year or any year, and the wonderful thing is that there is no possibility that their Tweets will be instantly shared and end up on millions of cell phones, computers, and iPads worldwide as breaking news. Nor will the Minnesota Tweets be sent automatically via the Internet to the Library of Congress to be stored forever.

Minnesota Tweets disappear into the air as soon as you use them.

Bob Humde's Cow Pie Key Hider Flops: An Update

The Bob Humde COW PIE KEY HIDERS, reality-based plastic replicas, are no longer manufactured. You can find them on eBay, where they are going for several dollars and have graduated to classic status in some areas of Wisconsin. Bob did not take into account the fact that his KEY HIDER was impractical for folks living in condos or apartments, or in spendy retirement facilities in Arizona whose rigid rules specify what front-door decorations are acceptable, and real or imitation bovine waste is not among them.

Personally, I think what really sank Bob's ship was the ORGANIC COW PIE KEY HIDER. The ORGANIC COW PIE KEY HIDER was indeed organic, in that it was formed and baked with a substance produced only by free-range cows and certified by the Department of Agriculture. You never know what the public will buy, but buy they did for a six-month period in 2005. The first ORGANIC KEY PIE HIDERS sold doubled in value every month, with people fighting over them at Walmart. Unfortunately after several exposures to rain, the ORGANIC KEY HIDER had a tendency to return to its original moist form, complete with some quite unsavory sensory problems and stains.

MINNESOTA FACEBOOK–DOUG'S STORY

According to Harold Mire, his first cousin Doug on his mother's side decided to quit one of his three bowling teams and get on Facebook because his "biological time bomb was ticking." He put up a photo of himself shingling the garage and his dog barking at the mailman. He wrote that he lived in a small southern Minnesota town, and his main hobby was bowling, though he really liked rebuilding old tractors about as much. Doug waited day after day in front of his computer for someone to friend him. In desperation, Doug contacted Facebook and explained what was happening and that he was very disappointed and somewhat depressed and didn't the company have a guarantee of some kind?

A Facebook counselor told Doug on the phone that Facebook was not responsible for getting him friends, and in fact the company was not required to do anything it didn't want to do, which sounded pretty harsh to Doug, so the counselor said if he wanted the Facebook corporation itself to friend him, it could do that now that the United States Supreme Court had ruled that corporations are people, and thereby can be frienders.

Being friended by Facebook itself broke the ice for Doug, and he was soon friended by Wells Fargo, Bank of America, Dial soap, Walmart, Sears, Ford, and GMC. Doug did not accept GMC as a friend because it would've been like treason for a lifetime Ford guy to be pals with an organization that made the Chevy. John Deere friended him later that day, opening up the chance to talk tractors till the cows came home.

A couple of months after Doug went on Facebook, Harold asked him if any women had showed interest in him on the site, since that was the original idea. "Nope, unless you count the nice lady from Dial soap. She asked me how many times a week I showered, which I thought was kind of intimate."

And then a week later Doug told Harold that his high school classmate Bock Joman tried to friend Doug and said he hoped they could forget the past. Ha! Doug knew that he would never forget the day Bock borrowed his mint 1949 Ford their senior year at Fremson and shelled out that great little V-8 engine at 110 miles per hour, locked up the tranny, skidded into a ditch, and rolled twice. After declining Classic Bock the Jock's friend request, Doug was cheered up when Lay's Potato Chips, the San Francisco Opera company, and the NRA friended him.

PRAIRIE ROAST
Soybean Coffee

All you want in a coffee
without all you don't want in a coffee

In taste tests across the country, **PRAIRIE ROAST SOYBEAN COFFEE** was chosen by blindfolded people two to one.

"I couldn't believe it. I picked **PRAIRIE ROAST SOYBEAN COFFEE**? It's good, it really is. I have to admit it. I guess I'm gonna go with soybeans from now on."

—Rosie, Des Moines

Drink **PRAIRIE ROAST SOYBEAN COFFEE** till your teeth float. Every cup of **PRAIRIE ROAST** will taste like your last.

For full, rich, heavy-bodied soybean flavor, use a **MR. SOYBEAN** automatic drip machine.

(Adv.)

Lesson 5

Dining Out in Minnesota

Minnesota has a rich tradition of native and foreign foods, and dining out is something we do whenever we feel like it. But if you expect the kind of dining experience you might have in Ohio or Montana, you'll be disappointed. You get what we have when you eat in Minnesota. It's always been plenty good enough for us, so it should take care of your needs, too.

In certain urban areas of Minnesota, there are citizens who read magazines from the East in order to learn the kind of manners that will take them to the top. But this group is a minority and keeps to itself. They like to dress up when they have the big lunch. This lets the rest of us (who are in the restaurant for dinner) know that our credentials are not in order and maybe we should have our wardrobe evaluated besides.

So if you're from a place where people put on impractical clothes in the middle of the day and have lunch, you'll be able to find some people to keep you company, but be warned that they are proud of being strangers in their own land of 10,000 lakes. You can do a lot better. But do what you want. Just don't come crying to me when you find out how dry they are.

Let's get one thing right out in the open about Minnesota restaurant dining. How much should you tip? Well, not too much, really. It's better to tip too little. A big tip only creates suspicions.

When it comes time to tip, after you've got the leftovers squared away in clearly marked doggie bags, you should discuss the amount with the others at the table. It's expected. Simply dropping the tip on the table without mentioning the total or reviewing how you arrived at it is bad manners in Minnesota.

—"Now wait a minute, did you have cottage fries, Tim?"

—"No, that was Donna. I had the dipped walleye."

—"Oh, yeah. The DW. And then here I am. And Patty, you're the steak sandwich, right?"

—"No, I'm the BLT, with onion rings."

—"Got it. Three milks, a Diet Coke. What's this here? It looks like 3*bS*."

—"Three-bean salad, I had a bowl of it."

—"Well, my total is the same as theirs. What do you say, 10 percent?"

—"Sure, why not. The food was good."

—"Maybe 15 percent then?"

—"It wasn't that good. My steak had some red in it."

—"So that's gonna be $2.33."

—"I've got the 33."

—"Let's just round it off to two bucks."

[*Note*: Tip only where you see this sign displayed: TIPPING ACCEPTED HERE. If there is no sign, don't tip, or you will be chased down the street by the waitress returning your money. As a rule, small-town cafés frown on tipping. If you tip, you're saying that you know more about the price of the food than the owner does. If the beef commercial plate is $2.95, it's $2.95. —H.M.]

Some restaurants will ask you how you want your steak or roast. What they mean by that is, do you want them to slice it up for you in the kitchen or will you do it yourself? Myself, I like to have my steak cut up for me. Then it's all ready to stab with the fork and dip in the gravy. In no circumstances should you say "medium rare" or "rare," unless you don't mind the cook coming out to get a good look at you. They'll do it for you, but they'll make sure you understand they don't approve. *Well done* is the benchmark for steak in Minnesota. It's the way I like it. In fact, *well done* is the benchmark for most Minnesota foods. It gets rid of all the bacteria.

☞ ORDERING

Here's a typical exchange between waitress and customer. Individual items may vary, but the approach is standard.

WAITRESS: "So what's it gonna be then?"

CUSTOMER: "Oh, boy, I can't decide. How's the meatloaf?"

W: "It's been moving really good. A lot of people have been ordering it."

C: "What would you order if you were sitting here?"

W: "I've had the tacos Italiano. They're okay."

C: "I guess I'll go with the beef commercial."

W: "Anything to drink?"

C: "What you got?"

W: "Milk, water, or pop."

Wine or beer is only served at night in most Minnesota restaurants. If you want the native wines, ask for the hearty rutabaga burgundy or the soybean chablis. Your wine will be served with ice cubes unless you request something different. When you toast somebody, you should hold up your glass and thump it with your index finger and say:

—"Well."

MINNESOTA SPICES

The three workhorses of Minnesota cooking are salt, pepper, and ketchup. If the ketchup bottle is not already on your table, the waitress will bring it automatically. The last customer probably used it all. We use ketchup like it was water.

FEED

Phrases

✓ *Feed cap*
✓ *Seed cap*
✓ *Off your feed*
✓ *Smelt feed*

The word *feed* gets quite a bit of mileage in Minnesota. Most of its uses relate to food and eating, both human and animal.

The hard pellets that smell like dead fish you pour into the cat's bowl are called cat *food*. And unless your cat lives inside the house—which I think is a ridiculous thing to do with a cat— the pellets are also skunk food, groundhog food, dog food, rabbit food, and bird *feed*. Whatever wanders by. Don't forget to change the water.

—"This cat food has tiny bugs in it. Should we buy a new bag or do you think the cats'll care?"

Mine don't.

If you raise cattle or hogs, the stuff you feed them is *not* called cattle food or hog food. It's called cattle feed or hog feed. You are feeding those animals feed to make them into human food—they are destined to become steaks and pork chops. It's a funny system, but you get used to it after a while and hardly think of it unless your animals have individual names. Where the cows and hogs live is in the feedlot.

NETBEGONE
EMERGENCY KIT™

WHEN THE GOING GETS TOUGH™

- Do you get out of bed in the morning and go directly to your computer in your jammies?

- Are you sometimes in your jammies at noon with your butt plopped on the chair in front of your computer?

- Do you download more than three new apps daily to your computer or other digital devices?

- As the e-mails and Tweets and attachments pile up, do you feel like an animal trapped in a net?

- Is your smartphone synced to your iPad and your computer?

- Do you wonder sometimes if you have a life?

- Has anyone ever told you to get a life?

- Do you sometimes feel totally ridiculous sending a Tweet or simply saying the word Tweet out loud in the presence of a sentient being, such as your spouse, or the retired Marine who lives next door?

- Has more than a year passed since you last wrote a letter in standard English and put it in an envelope and mailed it via the USPS to another human being?

If you answer YES to any three of the questions you need the NETBEGONE EMERGENCY KIT.* If you answer yes to all of these questions you need both the NEK and our wildly popular SCREENBEGONE KIT**

*The NETBEGONE EMERGENCY KIT cannot be described here without revealing our company's valuable intellectual property secrets. You will be pleased to know that no deaths or injuries have occurred with the use of either of these kits. For home use only to free you from the Net. You will continue to be netted at work.

**The SCREENBEGONE KIT also contains proprietary functions that are not all that violent in nature, depending on your personal threshold, but the kit should not be activated without clearing the area of children or folks with heart pacers. And once again, for home use only.

Order from our secure website, where your privacy is a big concern of ours.

Not available in California.

If you never get out to the country, none of this will matter to you. It may not matter to you anyway.

Cats and dogs are not raised for food in Minnesota, although outdoor cats and dogs sometimes tangle with animals bigger than they are and end up in about the middle of the rural food chain. It's a terrible deal, I guess.

What you feed the chickens is chicken feed. Chicken feed is basically the same the world over; it's what most people say they won't settle for. Chickens can make meals out of table scraps, crickets, spiders, worms, and can even thrive on the undigested portions of other farm animals' waste products. Chickens are good to have around—they're a walking lesson for us all.

The truck that delivers the cattle feed or the hog feed is called the feed truck and it comes from the feed mill. The truck driver will be wearing a feed cap.

Feed companies make feed, feed additives, and feed supplements that are mixed and delivered by the feed mill in the feed truck to the farmers with feedlots. The feed companies give free feed caps to all their customers. The name of the feed is on the cap.

Another cap worn here is called the *seed corn* cap. It is identical to the feed cap, except that there is a seed company's name on the front above the bill: Trojan, DeKalb, Pioneer, Funks, MPS—it's a long list. The seed companies sell alfalfa seed, clover seed, corn seed, soybean seed, and a few more besides. But the caps are never called seed soybean caps, or seed alfalfa caps. The seeds are planted and become feed for animals and food for human beings, or both.

A seed corn cap becomes nothing if it is planted.

Seed corn caps are available in summer or winter models—that is, with or without insulation and earflaps. One size fits all. Feed caps are unisex in style, although they are worn mostly by men.

People in or near the farming business in other states do wear feed and seed caps, it's true, but in Minnesota we have made it a matter of fashion. A Minnesotan may have only one suit and one pair of good black shoes to wear with it, but he will have a rack of feed caps divided into work and good. A good cap is not worn when you are out baling hay. That's for trips to town—after so many trips to town and so many removals, the good cap is shifted to the work pile. A work feed cap is worn until the bill falls off or your wife burns it.

A good clean feed cap can be worn anywhere at any time in Minnesota except inside the church during the service—keep it on your lap. It's okay to put it back on when the usher nods for your row to file out to shake hands with the minister. Members of the St. Paul Chamber Orchestra wear feed caps during their local performances. And a colorful and moving tradition during the Minnesota governor's inauguration is the transfer of the state feed cap from the old governor to the new. The legislators salute their new antagonist by lifting their feed caps in unison and give loon calls. Then they have a little lunch.

As in other parts of the country, funerals in Minnesota are either open or closed casket. But our other choice is with or without feed cap.

In Minnesota we know how to tie on the feedbag, we starve a fever and feed a cold, we feed our families, we feed the kids before we feed the adults, and we often have enough food at the table on Sunday to feed an army.

And if we can't eat, we say we are *off our feed*.

—"I'm sorry, Mabel, I'm gonna have to pass on the barbecues, I'm kinda off my feed today."

Off your feed is a phrase that comes from the feedlot, where when you inspect the feeder cattle to see how they're doing, you notice that one of the calves doesn't belly up with the others when you sling the feed into the bunker. That calf is off its feed and should be watched closely—if it keeps up, you may not be surprised some morning to find it lying on its back in the feedlot with four feet sticking straight into the air. Minnesotans who are off their feed rarely end up this way.

☞ THE PANCAKE FEED

Hardly a day goes by in Minnesota when you can't find somebody—a church, a VFW, a Boy Scout troop—who's putting on a feed. The most popular annual feeds are the pancake feed, the smelt feed, the lutefisk/meatball feed, the wild game feed, and the Rocky Mountain oyster feed.

What you get at a feed is all you can eat for a single price. It's a bargain if you're hungry. You sit at long tables covered with white paper and are elbow to elbow with your fellow eaters, some of whom have sharp elbows. Be careful who you sit next to—some people take the "all you can eat" sign as a personal challenge and tend to shower their neighbors with all manner of food particles and liquids.

The smelt feeds take place in the spring around the time of the smelt run in northern Minnesota, near Lake Superior. Smelt fishermen are known for their bravery—they will sit outside in the cold rain in the dark, get drunk, and then wade into a fast-moving stream just to catch a pile of smelt. But I guess it's worth it. Batter-dipped smelt can't be beat, especially with a plate of french fries, a little coleslaw, and a bottle of ice-cold beer.

The Rocky Mountain oysters do not come from the sea. They come from the feedlot via the pig. After the pig donates its oysters, it has a more laid-back outlook on life in the feedlot. Like smelt, they are generally batter-dipped and french-fried and eaten with relish.

Minnesota Summer Detours

In Minnesota we have spring, sometimes, but we have summer every time, and it is the very season when the powerful Bureau of Tourism has smoke coming out of its ears, and for good reason. Summer is the most lucrative season for lodge owners, bait shops, sports stores, restaurants, supermarkets, and casinos in "The Land of 10,000 Lakes." By actual count made in 2012 by a crew of recent college graduates living with their parents, there were 15,732 lakes, but "The Land of 15,732 Lakes" does not have the same ring to it. In any case, multitudes of out-of-state tourists make their annual migration up to their favorite lodge on their favorite lake, as they have been doing, sometimes for three generations or more. Summer unfortunately coincides with the road repair season of the Minnesota Department of Transportation (MnDOT).

Some out-of-state vacationers, mostly those from the East Coast, have been lost for up to three days on detours caused by MnDOT road repairs. What is most disconcerting to the Bureau of Tourism, apart from the tedious and expensive search parties involved, is that some of the vacationers accidentally wander into Wisconsin, North Dakota, and South Dakota and decide to stay and spend their tourist dollars there because they are sick of driving. One family from Cleveland heading for the Hide Yourself Lodge on Lake Winnibigoshish in 2007 ended up in Canada after missing two turns and following a farm field road that crossed the border with no customs stop on either side. Manitoba officials suggested that they might as well see the sights and do some fishing for Canadian walleyes because it was going to take a while to figure out how to get them back over the border without passports.

The Bureau of Tourism suggests to out-of-state tourists that they carry a cooler full of hydration supplies, sandwiches, two or three movies for the DVD player, and that they be prepared to stream movies on their iPhones and iPads as they wait for the stop-sign guy to rise out of his lawn chair.

In 2008 MnDOT, under new management, finally decided to beef up its reputation with the tax-paying public and untold vacationers from all over the USA by addressing the problem of lengthy detours. Nineteen-year-old video-game designer Gort and three of his gaming buddies with gaming degrees from a vo-tech were hired to create the detours.

Gort's team operated on the theory that the more complex the detours were, the more fun the drivers would have finding their way. The MnDOT gaming team won the coveted National Video Game Award for its STEALTH DETOUR in 2009, which included an overnight stay in a bat cave near Hinckley, a raft crossing of the Chippewa River, and a confrontation with Minnesota Bigfoot* before the drivers finally arrived up to the lodge on the lake. Visitors and Minnesotans alike gave the STEALTH DETOUR two thumbs down, and several bottoms up.

* Not a Minnesota Bigfoot juried sighting.

In the 2010 ROAD REPAIRS season, Gort's team tried to improve its ratings with the public by outdoing themselves on the outstandingly exciting WALLEYE WHIRLWIND DETOUR, in which three detours were intertwined so that vacationers from several states ended up in the parking lot of the Mall of America on the hottest day of the year. Minneapolis *Star Tribune*: WALLEYES NOT BITING AT MOA.

Gort was dismissed from MnDOT and was immediately hired to handle the interactive website for a well-known cell-phone provider whose name cannot be mentioned because it has a lot of lawyers on the payroll. Gort had much better luck there with his gaming expertise and penchant for hidden surprises, puzzling instructions, odd charges, satirical jabs at customers, and best of all, wild animations. It has been rumored that the next generation smartphone will be the GORT.

But it was back to the twentieth century for MnDOT in 2012, with long waits in the hot sun, steaming radiators, and fuming tourists. MnDOT did, however, begin handing out bottled water to any tourists who had to wait more than an hour for the traffic to move forward another car length. The bottled water came from China, another cross the Bureau of Tourism had to bear.

NOT SOLD IN STORES.

BY INVITATION ONLY.

THE TOUGH NATURAL CEREAL

Made from Oat Hulls and Wheat Chaff

My husband and I don't drive much, except at Christmas time. That's when we put 3,000 hard miles on our car driving to visit five states and fifteen different relatives. We spend *our* holiday in the car, they spend *theirs* looking out the window for us. In with the gifts, take our coats off, unwrap the gifts, watch them unwrap their gifts from us, coats on, out the door, and back on the road. Sometimes we leave the car idling out front, like bank robbers. We've got a little Christmas tree on the dashboard, and we take turns sleeping as we plunge through the night on icy roads. It's a Christmas tradition. And so is our cereal: *RAW BITS*. It's our gift to each other.

—J.H., St. Paul

SEND US YOUR RÉSUMÉ
and we'll let you know if you qualify.
Include two references.

Lesson 6

What to Say When You've Arrived

Phrases

- ✓ Yep
- ✓ Well?
- ✓ So?
- ✓ Greetings

When you travel to Minnesota, I hope you're not expecting to be met at the border by a bunch of hyper people in colorful clothing. Our black and white signs at the state line say it all: MINNESOTA. If a smiling group of people with colorful clothing does meet you at the border, lock the doors and don't get out of the car. They probably escaped from someplace.

Minnesotans do not favor the big hello. We do it, we just don't overdo it.

A few years back two brothers from Minnesota ran into each other at a highway restaurant near Alexandria. The restaurant keeps a picture of the brothers by the cash register. The eastern newspapers carried the story and used it as evidence that Minnesotans' obsession with winter was reflected in our manners and feelings—what they meant was that we were a cold people.

The two brothers—Frank and Gary—had not seen each other for sixty-four years, not since they were split up somehow on a Mississippi paddleboat. It involved a young woman from a river town and a girdle—and a catfish. I don't remember the exact details. They were twenty-two and twenty-three years old when that incident happened, whatever it was.

And then there they were at the restaurant in adjacent booths sixty-four years later. The waitress took Frank's order—he wanted a cheeseburger and a dish of chocolate ice cream. When she asked Gary what he wanted, he turned around in the booth, jerked his thumb toward Frank, and said, "I'll have what he ordered. Sounds good to me." And that's when he realized he was looking at his long-lost brother, and his brother realized the same thing at the same time. Gary said to the waitress:

—"It's my brother—I haven't seen him for over sixty years. Can I move my silverware over to his booth?"

This is how they greeted each other:

FRANK: "Well."

GARY: "Yep."

And that's all they said, according to the waitress, until Gary said:

—"Why don't you pass me the ketchup then, Frank?"

When they had finished their cheeseburgers, Frank said to Gary:

—"Should we just split the check down the middle then?"

Gary said:

—"Fair enough, even though you had iced tea."

Until you get used to the way we do things here, let's leave it that when you greet Minnesotans you don't jump up and down, you don't kiss them, you don't hold them in your arms. And don't advertise your emotional imbalance by saying:

—"I'm so happy to see you I can't stand it. Come here. Give us a big kiss."

You rarely see Minnesotans on TV game shows. We want a microwave oven and a new living room suite as much as the next person, maybe, but not if it involves throwing our hands in the air, squealing, and running down the aisle in a humorous costume.

I've never seen a Minnesota couple on *The Newlywed Game*. What those newlyweds say about each other in front of a few million viewers, a Minnesota man and wife would not say to each other in private, even after their fiftieth wedding anniversary.

We watch shows like that for the same reason we subscribe to the *National Geographic*.

The $64,000 Question was the last popular quiz show here. Minnesotans were drawn to the excitement of a person sitting in an isolation booth and concentrating.

When you visit a Minnesotan you know at home, you will be given the Minnesota greeting upon arrival.

—"So, then, it's you . . ."

Your reply should be simply:

—"You bet."

At this point, you may be given the Minnesota hug, which is the index finger at arm's length touching your shoulder briefly. Return it if you want, but nobody will be surprised if you don't, and won't care either.

If you arrive by car, the Minnesotan will likely be watching for you out the window with the curtains pulled to one side and will be out the door and in the driveway before you stop. You should roll down the driver's window so you can hear the greeting. A woman will say to you:

—"Want a little lunch?"

You should reply:

—"You don't have to go to all that trouble."

A man will greet you with:

—"How long you had this car?"

This is your cue to get out and open the hood and look at the engine. There'll be plenty of time to carry stuff in later.

The secret to the Minnesota greeting is to avoid the issue. When you meet somebody for the first time or for the fortieth time, start right off with:

—"I see you planted a sunburst locust in your yard."

Or:

—"My butt sweated the whole trip—I gotta get one of those cool-air cushions for the driver's seat."

If you are staying with Minnesotans in their home, don't be frightened by the mornings. We don't say "Good morning." And you should avoid saying it, too. Minnesota couples greet each other by staring. The first one to say "What?" completes the exchange.

 ## ARRIVING AT A HOTEL IN MINNESOTA

—"I'd like a room for two."

—"Is that your wife there?"

—"Yes."

—"Could we see two forms of ID?"

 ## WHERE TO GO IN MINNESOTA

Gambling

Although not widely advertised or encouraged, several forms of legal gambling do exist in Minnesota. If you know where to look when you visit, you can find some wagering action that might suit your taste. However, you should keep in mind that Minnesotans believe it is better to give than to receive, an attitude that can be counterproductive in gambling.

According to most theorists, the aim of gambling is to win. But most theorists have not taken into account most Minnesotans. If winning is your main goal in Minnesota games of chance, you may win, but you certainly will not be taken as a Minnesotan if you make too big a deal out of it.

Here is the classic statement on odds by Minnesota's most famous professional odds maker. It should give you a feel for Minnesota-style gambling.

Minnesota Odds

by Hans the Scandinavian

I had no idea what the odds were in the Burger Palace Bonanza Sweepstakes, and I didn't care, but out of seven stops for a root beer and a small fry, I won a fish sandwich one time and a bucket of chicken chunks another. That's pretty good luck, all right, and that could have worried me, but it didn't in this case because I don't like fish sandwiches—so that's a big zero—and the chicken chunks set off a gastrointestinal red-alert when I ate them, and so that win evened out. There I was back to neutral. It made me feel good.

The odds of winning the vacation home in the Bonanza Sweepstakes are about five million to one. I wouldn't mind having a vacation home, but I don't especially want to win it in a contest. Six homes will be given away in two styles. That means my chances of being killed in a car crash every year are the same as my chances of being the proud owner of a two-bedroom A-frame on a lake, with one and a half bathrooms. I don't like those odds, and if I had scratched off that silver stuff from the game card and seen a lake home instead of chicken chunks, I would've been depressed. You do what you want to, but if you ever win a lake home, I'd suggest you sit on your new redwood deck and watch people water ski. You could also play cribbage or gin rummy. I wouldn't drive around a lot. LOCAL MAN WINS LAKE HOME, PLUNGES OFF CLIFF IN STATION WAGON.

If you got tired of looking at the lake from your deck, you could take a plane someplace, because flying is way safer than driving, most people say, but you can tell that most people don't believe it.

What if you order a couple of magazines from Quonset Hut Subscription Service and end up winning a trip to Portugal, plus spending money, on a major airline? No telling what your odds were of winning that trip, but they were ridiculous, believe me, because nobody gives anything away. Your odds were roughly the same as your number coming up on the same flight. But don't let me discourage you. If you win, you have to go. How could you live with yourself if you didn't? Good luck. You'll need it.

When you flip a coin, the odds of calling the correct face are two to one no matter what system you use. If the odds of falling in the bathroom were two to one, most people would wait longer between showers. Most people will never fall in the bathroom, and those that do will rarely hurt anything but their pride, but I'm saying that without seeing your bathroom. What it boils down to is if you need to get something off your chest, you should consider doing it in the bathroom, even if you slam the door and throw aspirin bottles. The odds are a lot worse if you drive off down the road in a huff, unless your electric shaver has a short in it. But you shouldn't shave when you're angry anyway.

Most car accidents happen within twenty-five miles of home, for reasons that are not clear, but it sure is handier for everybody involved. If you take a long car trip, you can improve your odds by having someone pilot your car to the city limits. You should then take the bus out. Actually you should take the bus whenever you can. Very few people are injured or killed while riding a bus, even a city bus. The odds are someplace in the neighborhood of 500 million to one, but of course there is the chance you could be the one. There's always the chance. Stranger things happen all the time. But remember, you're statistically safer on that bus than you are in your living room, even if some loud punks take over the backseats and make threatening gestures. You could bring those punks home and hope they trip on your rug and hit their heads on the coffee table. It's a fairly good bet, as long as you stay seated on the davenport and the home you bring them to isn't the one on the lake you won in the Burger Palace contest.

Most people think that odds build up, that the more times something doesn't happen, the better chance it will happen the next time, and vice versa. I subscribe to this theory myself. If the favorite at Canterbury Downs comes in first in every race for a week, the bettors who believe in "odds pressure" will at some point the next week bet everything they have on Washday Blues, who placed a couple of years ago on a muddy track. If you haven't cut your finger lately slicing the roast, or worse yet, if you have never cut your finger slicing the roast, you should stop slicing roasts for a while to relieve the odds pressure. According to mathematicians, every time you carve a roast the odds of cutting your finger are the same, but if that's true why do mathematicians periodically switch to ham?

Avoid the long shots is my advice. If you happen to win something in a contest, even if it is only a set of luggage with somebody else's initials on it, your odds of winning were poor.

The plain fact is that the universe does not like people throwing things off balance. Somebody has to win, you might say. But it doesn't have to be you, I say. As everyone knows, if something good happens to you, then something bad has to happen. If apparently out of the blue a bad thing happens, you might wonder what you did to deserve it. Quite simply, something good happened to you that you didn't notice, and the universe was settling accounts.

After you open the registered letter from *Reader's Digest* that says you have won $50,000 a year for life, avoid running out the front door of the house screaming, "I won!! I won!!" The odds of your making it to the sidewalk before being struck by lightning or blown away by a tornado are not good. But you never know. If you have that feeling in your bones, go with it. But don't say I didn't warn you.

Where to Gamble

✓ *Deep Woods Casino*

[Reprinted with permission from the booklet published by the Gaming Division of the Minnesota Department of Natural Resources.]

You bet. Casino gambling in Minnesota. We've got it if you know where to look. And where to look is in the lake country of northern Minnesota. That's where the Gaming Division of the Department of Natural Resources has erected the one and only Minnesota casino.

When the state coffers went empty and began to fill up with IOUs, the governor of Minnesota felt that casino gambling could be the answer, but he felt it should be a beautiful and natural experience and therefore should not take place in an environment of luxury, where you would be surrounded by overdressed people with big rings.

The governor also felt that if people wanted to do some casino gambling they should have to work for it. Business consultants from out of state recommended that Minnesota's one and only casino should be located near Minneapolis and St. Paul, the population center of the state. That way more people could gamble and more money would end up in the state treasury, they advised. The governor said that making it easy for a whole bunch of people to gamble was not his intent.

With the blessing of the legislature and the major Minnesota churches, Deep Woods Casino was built on an island in the middle of Balloon Lake, north of Duluth. It can only be reached by canoe, it takes two days to get there, and you have to portage three times and shoot a rapids. It's a beautiful trip. Take your time paddling and you'll have your limit of walleyes before you ever say "Deal 'em."

The Deep Woods Casino is the biggest tent casino in the world, with one hundred campsites, modern pit toilets, and plenty of snowmobile parking in the winter. If you have the urge to gamble during your visit to Minnesota, get back to the basics. Ask your travel agent about a Deep Woods gambling canoe trip. It's gambling the way nature intended it.

[*Note*: Here are some sample dialogues for those interested in Minnesota-style casino gambling. Don't ask where I got the dialogues. Let's just say that it was a fun trip and I recommend it. —H.M.]

✓ On the Lake

—"Ah, smell that air, Ralph. We're miles from nowhere."

—"Have you ever seen lake water so clear, Rich? And those loons are music to my ears. Sure beats the deadening throb of the city, huh?"

—"I hooked another one. If it's a walleye, Ralph, I've got my limit."

—"It's a walleye, all right. Must be four pounds. Bring her in and then we'll head back to camp and have ourselves a fish dinner."

✓ Later, in Camp:

—"Good meal, good cigar, campfire. What more could a guy want?"

—"Gambling, Rich. That's what's missing. What say we change our flannel shirts and paddle over to the Deep Woods Casino for a little blackjack?"

—"Great. I could use the exercise. How far is it?"

—"It's about two hours if we hustle. We've gotta portage twice. Better bring the beef jerky."

✓ Inside the Deep Woods Casino:

—"That polka band's hot, isn't it? How's blackjack goin', Ralph?"

—"I'm up a little, no problem. Say, dealer, could you move that lantern closer? I can't read your cards."

—"You bet. Where you boys from?"

—"We're camped on Red Shoe Lake."

—"Nice lake. How're they bitin'?"

—"Caught a four-pound walleye around noon today."

—"Sounds good. Think I'll canoe on down on my day off."

—"How about we take in the casino show before we leave, Rich?"

—"Is it Sinatra?"

—"No, it's what's-his-name that plays the saw and tells Norwegian jokes. They say he's pretty good. He's got a girl in his act that whistles through her nose."

—"It'd be a shame to miss that."

A SINCERE WORD FROM
"FRIENDING GALORE"

FRIENDING GALORE is a convenient one-stop friending service that provides all manner of frienders for you, up to ten friends for a low introductory monthly charge of $32.95. When you apply online, give us your age (must be at least eighteen), medical history, church affiliation, current address, food allergies, gender, hobbies, and anything else you wish to share.* In less than four hours a real person at FRIENDING GALORE will choose and adapt your new virtual friends and send them to your Facebook account at the speed of light. All FG friends are guaranteed not to make trouble for you, or try to borrow money, and if they develop annoying habits, no problem for our software techs.

Betty, from Mesa, Arizona, says: "FG friends are better than real and don't get in a huff if you forget their birthday!" (Yes, for a small charge FG will give you all of your new friends' birthdays and will remind you when one is coming up.)

FG has an exhaustive list of virtual friends available from all walks of life, including astronauts, public accountants, stand-up comedians, high-steel construction workers, TV weathercasters, c-store clerks, x-treme snowboarders, high school queens, bond brokers, car mechanics, and hedge-fund managers. We modify their personalities to suit YOU, our customers, so that the bonding process will be accelerated.

K. L. of International Falls, Minnesota, the cold capital of America, likes us: "The best part about FRIENDING GALORE is how if you get tired of a friend, you can remove him/her with two clicks and have no regrets. There is a five-dollar dumping charge for each removal, but that's nothing compared to the emotional cost of giving the heave-ho to a real person, believe me."

*Download our privacy statement for further details. But be assured that your personal information will be safe with us, so go ahead and give us your Social Security number for your own peace of mind.

Talking Cars in Minnesota

 **CAR REPAIRS**

No matter how long you plan to hang around Minnesota, you'll probably be driving a car at some point, because most places in Minnesota can't be reached by anything else, except a boat. Which means there's a good chance you'll have car trouble while you're here. It's never been explained to my satisfaction, but most car trouble happens on vacation—serious trouble, I mean. Therefore, you should know the rudiments of dealing with a Minnesota auto mechanic. When I say "auto mechanic," I use the term loosely. We're talking potluck here—beggars can't be choosers. The oil pan isn't gonna fall off where it's handy for you, for sure, and if you think you're lucky because it happens near an oil station—forget it. It's the worst one in the area. Either that or it happens on the freeway and the tow-truck driver drags you and your car to what he calls the best place in town and when you get there, you notice cobwebs all over the tools and a sign that says: YOU DON'T TAKE NO CAR AWAY FROM HERE UNLESS YOU PAY IN CASH—NO EXCEPTIONS. Minnesota is full of good car mechanics and if you ever break down near my place, just give me a ring and I'll send you to the best—in fact, one of the best wrote the Foreword to this guide. But the car hardly ever bites the dust near a good one. I've been rooky-dooed a couple of times on the road. It can spoil a guy's vacation.

Here is a sample dialogue. You can practice further by inventing other car-repair problems for yourself.

DRIVER: "Warm, isn't it?" (Or: "She's cold, isn't she?" Depending on the season.)

MECHANIC: "You got that right. Humidity."

If the mechanic doesn't say anything else immediately, don't press him. This is the role he has been waiting to play since the last poor tourist rolled in. He may keep working on the car in front of him, he may go get a cold drink, he may seem to ignore you. He'll get to you—just hold your horses. After what may seem to you like enough time has passed to drive to the cabin and have your first beer, the mechanic will finally make his move.

MECHANIC: "Problems with the Buick?"

DRIVER: "If it's not too much trouble I thought maybe you could look at this thing. It's a Ford."

M: "Right. Ford. So what's it doing then?"

You should offer an opinion to give the mechanic something to work from, but don't act like a know-it-all.

D: "I don't know. Drive shaft, you think?"

M: "Did she kinda squeak?"

D: "Yeah, and shimmied sort of."

M: "I suppose a guy could check that drive shaft."

D: "Whatever. You're the boss."

M: "Why don't you run her in that second stall there."

D: "You bet."

If the mechanic mentions the word *transmission* or *crankshaft*, well, what can I say? You're down to two choices—you can sell the car to him or you can start signing traveler's checks.

I'm not saying this problem is worse in Minnesota than it is anywhere else in the country—it's just not any better.

👉 CARS IN CONVERSATION

Nothing will label you a stranger here faster than a shyness or ignorance about cars. Always keep in mind that cars are not just a means of transportation in Minnesota, they're a way of life and a top-rated subject of conversation among Minnesota men. You can talk to a Minnesota man about almost anything, but if you don't talk cars, the dry spells will be longer than usual.

Here's a typical conversation between two Minnesota men.

—"Read any good books lately?"

—"You bet."

—"What was it?"

—"A paperback."

—"Any particular paperback?"

—"Yeah, it was."

—"Men's fashions sure seem to be changing quite a bit, don't they?"

—"Not that I've noticed."

—"This acid rain business, I don't know what to think."

—"Me either."

—"What are you driving these days?"

—"Well, I still got that 1970 Chrysler Newport Special I bought used off a lot with 82,000 on it. She's been a good runner. It's broken in now with 164,000 actual miles on it. I ground the valves at 90,000, but otherwise I haven't touched it, except for some minor bodywork, you know, stuffing rags in the trunk holes where it rusted out, screwing a little sheet metal on the fenders. The usual. She's a little mushy in the brake area because of a slow leak in the vacuum booster—makes a noise like a whoopee cushion, but all you have to do is push harder on the brake pedal and it'll stop. Pushed so hard once I broke the back off the driver's seat. But I don't need a backrest anyway; it weakens your concentration.

"Back in August I took a wrong turn in the fog with the old Chrysler—I thought it was the road, but it was a farm lane and it headed right by the runoff area of this feedlot—must've been a hundred cattle in there. By the time my headlights reflected off that brown pool, I only had two choices: either gun it or skid to a halt in the middle and wade out. I gunned her and fishtailed through. Covered everything in the engine with about an inch of semi-liquid cow refuse—plug wires, distributor, fire wall. You name it. For about six weeks there until everything baked off, people would cup their hand over their nose when I drove by. A lot of cars couldn't take that kind of abuse. It's got that 386 V-8. The suspension system is hurting, though. I put heavy-duty shocks on her, but I've never been happy with the way it handles on the corners.

"I don't know what it is, but it'll start good—if you keep that manual choke I put on it out about an inch and motorboat the footfeed, but then she'll run ragged and then run good, and then cough and sputter for no reason I can figure. I'm guessing sticky valves, but it could be a bad plug wire. I can live with it. I just don't go more than thirty miles from home so I can phone my wife to get me if it cashes in on me.

"But it's been one thing after the other this last week. Turn signals failed. Not failed exactly. The lights lit up, but they didn't blink. So I have to blink them by flipping the lever with my left hand when I want to turn, which is okay, only for some reason that makes the radio go on and off in time with the turn signal. So I crawled under the dash, looking for a short, and it's spaghetti under there, and I cut a few wires, and taped some wires, and ripped out a couple of things that didn't look important. Turn signals work okay now, but when I turn on the radio, the windshield wipers go back and forth, unless the dome light is on. It's a mystery. I've been out there in the cold shop almost continuously for five days, standing on my head, trying to get to the bottom of it.

"But as I say, I can live with it, 'cause it's so cheap to drive. When my wife drives it, she wears dark glasses and won't wave at anybody. She says everybody knows that Chrysler and they laugh at her. But ever since I welded on that new homemade muffler at least it sounds like a truck now instead of a Boeing 727. She wishes we'd trade up to a '75 maybe or even a '78, she was saying. She calls the old Chrysler the prairie schooner, because it rides like a boat and steers like a raft. You gotta put up with a few inconveniences with an old car. That's my feeling. And if I had a newer car, you think it wouldn't have trouble? There's not a car made that doesn't require some creative maintenance."

If a Minnesotan asks you what you're driving, at all costs avoid the following kind of reply.

—"What? Are you kidding me? Who cares? I get in, I turn the key, I drive it. Period. That's it. If it's broke, I pay somebody to fix it. End of discussion. Let's talk about the bond market or something."

Minnesota women will also talk cars, but they mainly talk about men and cars together. The conversations can last awhile, but they usually begin like this:

—"Sometimes I wonder if he doesn't think more of that car than he does of me. He spends more time with it. He also caresses it more."

—"I know what you mean. And if you go out to the shop he says 'What?' the way he does."

—"My mother said I should watch out for other women. She didn't say anything at all about watching out for cars."

—"You bet. If Harold looked at another woman I'd take it as a sign of health."

—"You got that right."

 ## THE MINNESOTA FELLOWSHIP FOR CAR MECHANICS

It's no secret that Minnesota is the hotbed of artistic endeavor and the national leader in awards, grants, gifts, and stipends given to those with a flair for the creative arts.

But what is not so widely known is that self-made Minnesota millionaire and shade-tree mechanic, Orton Daily, is responsible for the world's first (and only as of this printing) Fellowship for Car Mechanics. When Orton died a bachelor in early 1970 (he was found with his head under the hood of a '49 Hudson, dipstick in hand and a smile on his face), his will directed that his entire fortune go to establish the Daily Oil, Gas, and Grease Foundation. He said he was "tired of seeing foundation money poured down a rathole" and he wanted some car mechanics to get in on the gravy train. "If it came to a choice, and your car was missing, would you want a poet to work on it or a mechanic?" To him the answer was obvious.

I asked Donald L. Ballade, Duluth, the 1986 recipient of the Minnesota Fellowship for Car Mechanics, to write a few words about his award:

It's not the twenty-five grand, you know, even though it's tax-free, that I was after. I wanted freedom to explore innovative ways to work on cars. When I was tied down to my 8-to-5 job—ha! I was lucky to get out of the shop by 7—I really didn't have the time or the energy to experiment.

So the first thing I did was travel to Europe for three months, where I studied foreign auto-repair techniques. When I got back I immediately started assimilating some of those ideas into my developing concept of the American tune-up. I meant to set the world of carburetion on its ear. I figured I could do that best by renting a beach house on Martha's Vineyard. There was an attached garage where I did my

Bob Humde

COMPOSTO-CARB

Bob Humde here for a chat about my COMPOSTO-CARB. It's the carburetor you always heard about that Detroit kept secret for years, but I built it. You just take the old carburetor off your car and attach the Bob Humde COMPOSTO-CARB. Then fasten down the rooftop supply bin with the two-inch lag screws. Then you scoop organic matter into the bin and from there it is suctioned through a plastic drainpipe into the COMPOSTO-CARB, where it's processed for combustion.

Use anything: lettuce, stuff from the back of the refrigerator, most of the garbage from your house, and all forms of animal waste. Just shovel your supply bin full every morning and you can run all day.

I've had a COMPOSTO-CARB on my Buick for six months, and what I like is, you don't have to worry about tailgaters. And if your bin runs low, just throw in anything. I drove from St. Paul to Duluth once on just dead animals I found along the road. And that's not the half of it. Every COMPOSTO-CARB comes with my personal 10,000-mile/-50-tons-of-waste warranty and one free fill with the waste of your choice.

work at night. During the day I did quite a bit of sailing to relax and to let my thoughts gel.

It was a good year for me. I went deeper into myself. When I opened my shop doors again, the customers were the big winners—I had found my identity as a contemporary mechanic, and they could tell it and had no objections to my raised prices. Next month I'm speaking to a group of car mechanics in Brainerd about attitude. And in the summer, I'll be leading a carburetor workshop at the car-repair retreat up on the North Shore.

TALKING CARS: AN UPDATE

The basic information for visitors to Minnesota about what to say to the mechanic if you have car trouble is still accurate, especially if you are driving a vintage car, that is, a vehicle from 1987 or before. But if you have hopped on the twenty-first-century bandwagon and now own a vehicle manufactured after 2002, your interface with any mechanic in Minnesota will be considerably different.

MECHANIC: "So what can I do you for then?"

OUT-OF-STATE VISITOR (OSV): "We're heading up to the Lost Walleye Lodge for a couple of weeks, and all of a sudden there's something's wrong with this thing, because the engine light came on and it's blinking."

MECHANIC: "You're in for a good time, because Lost Walleye Lodge is one of my favorites. No frills but lots of good vibes, as we used to say in the sixties."

OSV: "Well, yeah, thanks for the tip, but what about the blinking engine light on the dash?"

MECHANIC: "The deal is that engine light is not supposed to blink, so the first thing we know is that there's a problem with the check-engine light. It shouldn't blink."

OSV: "Big trouble?"

MECHANIC: "Your check-engine warning light, blinking or not, covers engine problems from *A* to *Z*."

OSV: "Can you help me?"

MECHANIC: "Pop the hood and I'll plug in the computer and see what we got. Of course it could be anything, in my estimation."

OSV: "Do you think it's something bad? You look worried."

MECHANIC: "A guy never knows. Here we go, here we go, the screen is coming up, take a look."

OSV: "Yeah, I see it says there's a malfunction in the check-engine light. Can you fix that?"

MECHANIC: "Nothing to fix the way I see it."

OSV: "Could it be the carburetor?"

MECHANIC: (hearty laughter) "It could be anything *except* that. You've got a fuel injection engine."

OSV: "So what should I do?"

MECHANIC: "You should get back in the car and continue on your way to the Lost Walleye Lodge."

OSV: "But is it safe to drive?"

MECHANIC: "It's safe to drive unless you keep obsessing about that blinking engine light and forget to pay attention to the road."

OSV: "Can you turn that light off for me?"

MECHANIC: "I don't have the codes for that, but I tell you what, I'll put this attractive piece of gray duct tape over that blinking light so you can't see it, and you're good to go."

OSV: "How much do I owe you?"

MECHANIC: "My professional consultation is on the house."

OSV: "Gosh, thanks."

MECHANIC: "You bet. Enjoy your stay."

PHONES

In 1997 my wife and I were holdouts, proud owners of rotary dial phones that worked via landlines: our service provider was "Reasonable Phone Company" (RPC) in southwestern Minnesota. Our phone bill averaged $23 a month and we had one phone on the hallway table and another hanging on the wall in the kitchen. Our phone number was listed in a phone book. If something went wrong, we would just call the RPC and they'd send out their local phone repairman, Clarence. Nice guy, and more than once he stayed for lunch if the problem was extensive. In 1997 our three children were ages seven, nine, and eleven and had phone privileges unless they abused the privilege by tying up the line. In 2000 we bought a computer because our kids needed it to do homework, or so they said, and pretty soon we had two lines, one for talking, the other for dialing up the Internet. I should've seen that coming. We were up to $46 a month for the phone and $35 a month for the Internet service. In 2002 we fell for the "in case of emergency ploy" from our sixteen-year-old with a driver's license and no after-school job to pay for his cell service that was $47 a month. Sorry, I'm pretty certain the RAW BITS company doesn't like whiners, so here's the deal: today in 2010 my son has graduated from college with an interdisciplinary degree and is now living at home. He has a smartphone, our two daughters have smartphones, and believe it or not our "phone" bill is now a media bill that often exceeds $270 a month, which includes my wife's smartphone. She says she needs to be in touch with the children, who communicate with the outer world only through texting. I am back to using the landline with a rotary dial desk phone, a feeble protest at best, because it runs $72 a month on top of the media bill. I am not asking for a bailout. I just want to qualify for RAW BITS because I have the feeling I'm gonna need it as the future keeps crashing in on me.

—S.H. (please omit my address)

Bob Humde Composto-Carb: An Update

The COMPOSTO-CARB is one of Bob Humde's most ambitious inventions. However, Bob's description of the COMPOSTO-CARB implies that the car operates solely on waste products, when actually he should have mentioned that it also has a gas tank and uses some petroleum for the combustion process. The ratio of low lead to waste was a very fuel efficient one gallon to three bushels in 1986, when Bob did the drive from St. Paul to Duluth. In other words, Bob Humde created the first hybrid car in Minnesota, with a fossil fuel efficiency that has not been touched since.

But as usual, Bob was a bit slack about consulting applicable regulations. It was soon after the Duluth run that Bob ran afoul of the Minnesota Pollution Control Agency (MPCA), two deputies of which dropped by his workshop west of Hanley Falls to test emissions on the hybrid Buick. The MPCA had been hearing complaints from several folks who had to follow behind Bob's hybrid on his historic trip, and from homeowners who lived along Bob's route.

I was not able to get my hands on a copy of the MPCA test results, but it was widely known that the phrase "stunk to high heaven" was used liberally in the scientific report. That was that for Bob. It took the wind right out of his sails.

The Minnesota Historical Society (MHS) acquired the hybrid Buick for an undisclosed sum in 1995. It had been sitting in the grove of trees behind Bob's house since his censure by the MPCA. It was restored to its original condition and is displayed in the main lobby of the MHS inventor pavilion, where it continues to be one of the most popular permanent installations.

Lutefisk

[*Note*: I'm sorry that I have to mention lutefisk (*lewd*-uh-fisk) in this guidebook. Sorry for myself. If I don't mention lutefisk the critics will jump me for the glaring omission, but if I do mention it, as I am doing right now, they'll jump me anyway for stooping to such a thing. But my obligation is to you, the reader. How can I let you travel to Minnesota totally ignorant about lutefisk? —H.M.]

lutefisk, n. [from OHG, *fishlute*, a banjo-like instrument played with the elbows.] 1. a translucent, rubbery food product with a profound odor, created by soaking dried cod in a solution of lye, although equivalent results are claimed for doing the same to gym socks. 2. *lutefiskicuffs*, an altercation between several Scandinavians over who gets the last slice. 3. [Rare] linear distance from the rock to the hard place. 4. [Slang] a two-door automobile with bald tires and no taillights. 5. [Poker] the biggest pot of the night, taken with a pair of deuces.

—from *The New Lutefisk Handbook*

ICE FISHING IN MINNESOTA

Here are some answers to Frequently Asked Questions about ice fishing, with answers from the Minnesota Bureau of Tourism booklet meant to lure visitors from Texas, Florida, and Arizona to Minnesota in winter.

1.1. **Why should I spend my vacation in Minnesota in the winter instead of the summer?**
Ice fishing is the answer. You won't get sunburn. The kids aren't gonna hound you to go water skiing. No detours, no road construction. All the fancy restaurants will be closed. No mosquitoes. No waiting for a tee time. Ice fishing is fishing as Nature intended it. The only sounds will be the snapping of your nose hairs as they freeze and thaw with each breath and the distant whisper of traffic headed for the casino.

1.2. **I kind of like the idea of leaving Tampa in the winter and driving up to do some ice fishing for walleyes, but down here the TV people always call Minnesota the "Frozen Tundra of the North."**
You must have seen that TV documentary about the town of Dunferg, Minnesota, a few years ago. Totally exaggerated. What happened was that an unexplained flash-freeze front went through the town and all seventy-three citizens of Dunferg were frozen stiff as boards. Unfortunate, yes, but we would rather focus on the positive aspects of the freak accident. The University of Minnesota's celebrated Department of Ice came out immediately and revived the victims with their breakthrough slow-thawing technology. Not one citizen suffered any permanent effects from the experience, except the mayor of Dunferg, who periodically barks like a dog at council meetings and eats all the doughnuts.

1.3. **What equipment do I need to get into ice fishing?**
At the basic level you need an ice auger for drilling the hole and a five-gallon plastic pail with a lid to sit on. The pail contains your beer, bait, and lunch. Tie the line to a short stick and attach your choices of sinker, bobber, and hook.

1.4. **How large should the ice hole be?**
Never bigger around than you are.

1.5. I'm a fly fisherman. What special casting techniques should be used for ice fishing?
Most guys lean over and drop the line in from about two feet above the hole. You will develop finesse after a day or two on the ice.

1.6. Do I really have to sit outside?
Personally, I prefer the pure form of ice fishing, but if you must have shelter, think small. If your fish house has upstairs bedrooms, fine art on the walls, flush toilets, attached garage, and you bought it through a realtor, you have sullied the sport.

1.7. What should I look for when I buy a fish house?
Make sure it has a door. Then make sure it has a window on the opposite side in case it tips over doorside down. For size, most guys like something that will seat five poker players.

1.8. Is ice fishing dangerous?
Driving your pickup in the dark onto a frozen lake thirty feet deep and parking it next to your fish house is statistically safer than watching three bowl games in a row on TV while eating junk food. Most guys make it a habit to drive only their oldest pickup onto the ice, and they keep the windows rolled down and don't wear their seatbelts.

1.9. Do Minnesotans really race their fish houses?
Not if they can help it. What caused that rumor was that about twenty-five years ago Roger Swenson gained notoriety after he fell asleep inside his fish house on Leech Lake. When he woke up, he was sailing across the ice pushed by a Canadian clipper out of the northwest. The sheriff figured he reached a good forty-five miles per hour by mid-lake, a fish house speed record that still stands.

2.1. I'm from New Jersey and I wonder if ice fishing would be a way to meet beautiful Minnesota women?
Well, yes and no. It's a bit tricky. Gender is very hard to determine when you're faced with hooded parkas, ski masks, wool-lined boots, heavy gloves, and insulated pants. We call it Ice Roulette.

2.2. I'm from Atlanta and what's this I hear about that professional wrestling governor of Minnesota you-all had a few years ago?
There is a lot to hear about him, but if you mean "Did he want to make ice fishing a sport involving skimpy tight costumes, masks, finger-jabbing, and top-of-the-lungs boasting?" the answer is no. But Jesse "The Body" Ventura did have pretty good luck making the job of governor a contact sport, as many a legislator learned the hard way. A bipartisan body slam was a very successful vote changer.

2.3. I live in Key West and I'm into extreme sports, so what's the rush in ice fishing for me?
The ice-fishing high comes only from sitting alone in the dark for hours on a frozen lake with no bites. Once you've experienced the ice-fishing ecstasy, scuba diving with sharks, and parasailing into the Amazon from ten thousand feet seem about as thrilling as driving into town to get 2 percent milk.

CHICKEN-FEATHER SIDING
Natural beauty for your home

Call CHICKEN-FEATHER SIDING today and cover your house with feathers tomorrow. Highly trained, courteous crews brush on a coating of tar and then use a powerful patented blower to plaster every square inch of your house with the attractive and protective warmth of chicken feathers. Thousands of satisfied customers can't be wrong.

"I am totally satisfied with the chicken feathers installed on my home. It doubled the value of my property."
—Tom F., Des Moines

"CHICKEN-FEATHER SIDING does not smell and it is very warm. I did not start my furnace last year. I am very happy."
—T. ("Guts") W., Moose Lake, MN

"I am totally happy with my CHICKEN-FEATHER SIDING—it does not have a bad odor except when it rains, and my kids love to pet the house."
—J.W.M., Cedar Rapids

"I'm from Texas and we get these terrible sandstorms, but my CHICKEN-FEATHER SIDING holds up real good. It ruffles a little in the wind, but so do I."
—J.G., Austin

"I bought wood siding for my house, and the termites ate it off. I bought steel siding and it rusted off. I bought vinyl siding and it melted in the sun and dripped off. Finally I bought CHICKEN-FEATHER SIDING and it stayed right on there. I am tickled pink."
—R.M., Philadelphia

CHICKEN-FEATHER SIDING
FEATHER-CLAD WARRANTY
—
**Requires no maintenance
except preening and waxing**

(Not available in New Jersey)

How We Write Our Poetry Here and What We Do with It

Poetry is just below corn as a state crop, and slightly above soybeans. Not much poetry is exported—most of it gets consumed one way or another by Minnesotans. As they say around here, if our poetry had any calories, we'd all be fat.

There are different opinions on the subject of Minnesota's poetic produce. My opinion probably doesn't matter, but I think a person could do a lot worse things than write poems, so I'm all for it. That doesn't mean some poets couldn't do a lot better.

I've tried to include here a representative sample of views on Gopher State poetry, not all popular views. When you visit, keep in mind another saying we have: you can try to ignore our poetry if you want, but it's not gonna go away by itself.

How We Write Our Poetry Here

by Grant Mentor, CEP

[*Note*: Grant Mentor is Chief Executive Poet of the Minnesota Prairie Poet League, one of the strongest forces in contemporary nature poetry in the world, with over 800 members (798 Minnesotans) and 2,300 books to date. At present Mr. Mentor is editing the League's long-awaited magnum opus—a twenty-volume work to be called *Ten Thousand Lakes: Ten Thousand Poems*. One of my poems—"School Grove Lake Educates Us All"—is scheduled for Volume 8, as long as I keep paying my dues to the League, which I plan to, although I would feel better about it if Grant hadn't raised his salary this year. —H.M.]

The Minnesota Prairie Poet League Oath:

I pledge to memorialize Minnesota nature in poetry,
without regard for monetary gain or personal safety.

Let's lay our poetic cards on the table. We believe that if a poet moves into a small farmhouse on the Minnesota prairie and is unable to produce a collection of nature poems, he or she should go back to where he or she came from. All of us in the Prairie Poetry League have nurtured our talents on the prairie, and even though some of us have moved to the city and bought condominiums in order to be closer to the office, nature never leaves our hearts.

The key is sincerity. Nature abhors pretense.

Let me speak personally here for a moment. Before I put in my formative year on the prairies, I was a typical urban scribbler, obsessed by shopping malls, diesel fumes, and pavement. I wrote good poems, even a fairly well-known sonnet cycle on downtown redevelopment. And that's not to say that the city isn't fit for poetry: the inhuman crush of people, the explosive frustration of one-side parking in the winter, runaway crime, and singles bars must have their voice, but that voice is prose, not poetry.

I remember my very first day in the farmhouse (I found it in the League's newsletter: "Old fmhse, lbdr, lvngrm, wdbrngstve, 2cmpsothps, no rnngwtr. Must sacrifice, going to NYC") when I looked out the west window of the kitchen and wrote what became the central poem in *Snow Piles* (Gopher Press). The prairie, indeed, spoke to me immediately, and it kept on speaking through the winter.

On the first day it spoke of silent shadows ("Scared"), animals at dawn ("What's That Gnawing Sound?"), small flying bugs ("The Bug in My Ear Is Saying Hello"). On the second day the prairie said I must create my own mountains in a land so flat only the grain is elevated ("Higher Truth"). On the third day it told me I would never get hot water unless I turned on the propane tank ("Fossil Fuels"). The next day it told me I had to light the water heater myself, but I couldn't, so I called Prairie Propane and they sent a man out ("Fire Bringer").

Snow Piles grew naturally out of a prairie winter, where I asked myself many questions. Why does it seem colder after lunch? Will TV reception be better if I put the antenna on the chicken house? Is it okay to have the lead-in wire horizontal? Should I invest in a signal booster? I loved walking down the lane to the mailbox ("Rural Free Deliverance"). One letter addressed to Current Occupant could generate an afternoon of excitement. Whether I wanted to borrow $5,000 on my signature from a loan company in Pittsburgh or not, I read the brochure until I understood it completely ("It Looks Like a Good Deal").

Out there in the farmhouse, I came to realize that there is no such thing as an accident for a nature poet—everything, no matter how small, is charged with meaning if we can only see it. One day, after two weeks of below-zero weather, I took my Datsun a mile down the road and ran over a large object and blew out a tire. It was a deer's head with antlers ("Deer Tracks and Other Traces"). How strange, how wonderful.

And there was that morning when I stood in the yard and watched my neighbor's house moving slowly from north to south. Where was he going? Why was he taking his house? Was that his wife waving from the picture window? Was this a holiday? I never saw them again.

Enough about me and my first book. If you have that poetic drive, drop by the Prairie Poet League's headquarters in the IDS tower. After your interview and standardized test, we'll get you settled. And don't worry about the relocation fee. We've got a payment plan to suit every budget.

Oh, for and Heckuva Deal

Phrase

✓ *Oh, for*

The *oh, for* construction is used mostly by women to describe a person, thing, or animal, including oneself. For example, if a kitten climbs into somebody's shoe, you would say *Oh, for cute.* If the baby smiles and waves its arms, you would say *Oh, for darling* or *Oh, for sweet.*

If you were supposed to bring the Jell-O/pineapple salad to the potluck and you forgot it, you would say

—"Oh, for dumb."

If you are attending a bridal shower and the bride-to-be has just unwrapped a lace nightgown, you would say

—"Oh, for nice."

If the bride-to-be receives a ten-piece Tupperware set, including the lettuce keeper, you would say

—"Oh, for useful."

If somebody accidentally unplugs the refrigerator and a gallon of melted chocolate rocky road ice cream is spreading across the kitchen floor when you get back from the dentist, you would say

—"Oh, for yucky."

If you are at League Bowling and your ball leaps the gutter into the next lane, you would say

—"Oh, for embarrassing."

Men do not use the *oh, for* phrase in the same way. If the mechanic at the garage shows you the grease all over the brake shoes, it would be a big mistake for a man to say

—"Oh, for dirty."

On the other hand, both men and women in Minnesota will say

—"Oh, for crying out loud!"

when one of the kids says she ran over the lawn mower with the car, but the tire can probably be patched.

 # THE MINNESOTA DEAL

Phrases

✓ *Heckuva deal*

✓ *Good deal*

The word *deal*, in combinations such as "It's no big deal," has no more to do with gambling than *you bet*. The *deal* phrases are used to express a Minnesotan's range of feelings and opinions. Study this exchange between two Minnesota males.

—"Martha and I are having a few people over for steaks on Sunday. We hired a band. You're invited, not that you have to come."

—"What's the deal?"

—"It's no big deal."

It's not too good a deal means almost the same thing as *It's a bad deal*, depending on who's speaking and what the trouble is.

—"I went up to the lake last weekend—heard the walleyes were biting—and the motor got loose and fell into about a hundred feet of water. I knew I shoulda tightened those clamps."

—"That wasn't too good a deal."

—"It was a bad deal, all right."

Don't confuse *It's a bad deal* with *Not too bad a deal*, which means almost the same as *It's a good deal*, depending.

—"Listen to this. I got a raise on Friday, then Saturday I hit a long shot at the track. Cool Whip came in at 40 to 1. Not too bad a deal, huh?"

—"You bet. Good deal."

Quite the deal means it's a *pretty good deal*, only a little more, depending.

—"Say, I heard you took a trip to Europe."

—"You bet."

—"How was it?"

—"It was quite the deal."

—"Sounds like a pretty good deal to me."

Good deal can be dropped in a conversation anyplace and it can be interchanged with *you bet* for variation. No matter what anybody says to you in Minnesota, you can reply with "Good deal."

—"Well, going to the state fair was different this year."

—"Good deal."

Of course when *good deal* is used this way it doesn't mean that it was a good deal necessarily. In this case they were all doing fairly well through Machinery Hill and the Sheep Barn, but then they ate a bunch of Pronto-Pups and Mini-Donuts before they rode on the Tilt-a-Whirl. What did they expect?

More practice: Just say "Good deal" after each statement until you sound completely neutral and semiconscious.

—"I'm not gonna start you as center tonight, Bill, you've been falling down too much on the court."

—"Looking at your transcript, Carol, the only course that transfers is General Math. You basically have another four years ahead of you."

—"Sir, I'll seat your party at this table near the kitchen exhaust fan."

—"We decided to stay with you and Helen a couple more days. We're not doing anything at home anyway, now that Mack's out of work."

Now go back to the practice statements and say "You bet" after each one. See how upbeat it sounds?

Now do the same with *whatever*. As you can see, *whatever* is a more strongly opinionated reply than *good deal* in these examples.

For further practice, pick up a romance novel and read a passage of dialogue out loud, substituting *good deal* and *you bet* for the speeches of one character.

—"Oh, God, Jacques, I can't stand it when you do that."

—"Good deal."

—"I don't ever, ever want you to leave. You won't leave, will you, Jacques?"

—"Good deal."

—"Oh, Jacques, say it, say it—I've got to hear it from you."

—"You bet."

A *heckuva deal* is the biggest deal of all in Minnesota.

—"On that Oldsmobile of mine, you know, I'm gettin' about thirty-two miles to the gallon *in town*. Not too a bad a deal, huh?"

—"That's a heckuva deal if you ask me."

Caution: Don't confuse *a heckuva deal* with *a heckuva note*. A *heckuva note* is never *a heckuva deal*—it's closer to a *bad deal*.

—"I didn't notice my credit card was missing and somebody bought this big stereo system and the company says it's my problem."

—"Well, that's a heckuva note."

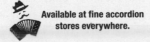

Polka Pants™

Carl Griscowski, CEO of POLKA PANTS, LLC, and the patent holder for POLKA PANTS, was a big fan of the *Polka Hour* from its beginning in 1968 on his local PBS channel in south central Minnesota. Both Carl and the *Polka Hour*, I'm happy to say, are still kicking in 2012. The *Polka Hour* is a raucous free-for-all featuring regular folks from near and far in Minnesota who love to polka and don't mind having people watch them dance with their sweethearts. Carl loved the way the women whipped their polka skirts around with no unsightly pulling and binding when they danced, but the men seemed drawn to the polyester pants that had no wiggle room. It cramped their style big-time, especially after they grew larger in the middle and the polyester pants did not, which inevitably resulted in the tremendous on-camera steamy blowouts that sent entrepreneur Carl to the drawing board. By the early 1970s POLKA PANTS were available in accordion stores nationwide. Turk and the Oompah Turkeys in 1974 was the first polka band to switch over to wearing POLKA PANTS on the bandstand, but not the last.

Carl made a bundle on POLKA PANTS, retiring to Florida in 2006, where he streams the *Polka Hour* on his laptop every Saturday afternoon. Carl turned the company operations over to his son, Noah, in 2008. In 2010 Noah moved the POLKA PANTS factory to China from its original location in New Ulm, Minnesota. In early 2011 the first shipment of twenty-thousand pairs from China arrived with POKER PANTS emblazoned on them.

Noah said it was a fluke. He managed to break even by selling the POKER PANTS to the Federal Prison System. POKER PANTS are a hot item on eBay, the only way to get a pair unless you are convicted for grand theft auto or armed robbery.

Lesson 11

Your Winter Vacation in Minnesota

Winter vacations in Minnesota are pretty popular because of the many recreational opportunities, including ice fishing and snowmobiling. Winter is not so bad here, really. The stories in Sunbelt newspapers about tourists who have disappeared and been found unspoiled during the spring thaw are exaggerated. Sure it's happened, but what's a vacation without a little risk?

Heartwarming Human Interest Stories from Minnesota Blizzards

(reprinted by permission from assorted state newspapers)

[*Note*: It seems as if winter brings out the best in people. Another good reason to make your trip in the winter. —H.M.]

Good Samaritan Delivers Lutefisk

A Minneapolis man skied two miles, slogged three, and crawled several hundred yards through deep snow to deliver four pounds of lutefisk to Mr. Ole Olson of St. Paul, who had been unable to pick up his order at the lutefisk depot before the storm hit. The unidentified man, who lives in the white frame house in the 1400 block of Beebee Boulevard, said he wants no thanks, the deed was reward enough. Apparently the elderly Olson offered to cook up a mess of the slick, shiny fish for the Good Samaritan, but according to Olson, the man said he felt invigorated after the exercise and he wasn't all that hungry, he would pass on the lutefisk. Later Ole Olson ate most of the lutefisk himself, with a special cream sauce made from cabbage and a pinch from a plug of Old Socks snoose.

Local Man Gets Faith Restored

A local man, Larry Gavene, was pleasantly surprised after the blizzard this week when he dug his late-model car out of drifts in the parking lot where he works and discovered a note from a would-be felon on the front seat. "Your stereo, your tapes, and the fuzzbuster are right there where they're supposed to be because it brought tears to my eyes to think of you shoveling and shoveling and then finding your stereo system gone. I took one of your candy bars from the glove compartment and left a quarter. I also hotwired the car so I could warm up. I appreciate it sincerely. God bless you in the coming year."

When Mr. Gavene arrived home he found another note on the closet floor where his case of twelve-year-old Scotch had been. The penmanship was familiar. "This you can do without. Sorry about the relapse. I'd be the first to admit that we need some changes in the criminal justice system. I'm a hopeless case, probably, although you never know—with the right support network I could turn over a new leaf. Once I got your address from the registration card I just had to see what kind of house you lived in, and sure enough, nice place, but one suggestion: repaint the dining room in a pastel. By the way, I took the gold coins you had in that cute little safe made from a hubcap under the false floor below the kitchen sink. I give you a B-plus for effort. Many happy returns and let me say, I have no hard feelings about any of this, if you don't. It happens, Larry, it happens."

Mr. Gavene said it could have been "a lot worse" and it was a pleasure in a way to deal with a polite and literate thief for once.

DJ Goes Berserk, Hauled In

As the blizzard picked up steam on Wednesday, Mike "Speedboat" Arntsen, well-known Twin Cities radio personality, allegedly "had it up to here" with reading school- and business closing an nouncements. Arntsen had logged over 4,000 announcements, including 540 late starts and no morning kindergarten, when—according to KRED chief engineer D. Dwight—he threw the list into the air and got a "strange look" on his face. Speedboat opened the Yellow Pages of the phone book and closed everything from Aardvark Beauty Shoppe down to Millicent's Rent-a-Fantasy before being put under house arrest by special agents of the Federal Bureau of Radio Ethics. Arntsen entered a plea of "temporary insanity" and was released on his own recognizance.

Area Farmer Sent Kiting During Storm

A farmer in the hard-hit southwestern part of Minneapolis had a ride he won't soon forget. When the blizzard struck, in early afternoon, Jody Ethleton was in his ice-fishing house and decided to stay put because the walleyes were biting, so he just packed himself another pipe and turned the oil burner up a notch. About sundown, according to Ethleton, the fish house was propelled across the frozen lake by the seventy-mile-per-hour winds. "I could feel it shudder and I thought, well, it's going over, but it didn't. She sort of accelerated and it was smooth sailing after that, mostly, with some short stops when the wind let up, but I wasn't about to open the door." Ethleton was found the next morning by a search party of neighbors. By then he had his limit of walleyes (in the two-pound range) but his tobacco was gone.

Helpful Cop Gets Last Laugh During Blizzard

Dorset Andersen, town constable in Boxelder, was sitting in his office watching *Hogan's Heroes* when a woman called and said she was starting labor and she was alone ten miles out in the country and the car wouldn't start, and besides, it was snowed in. Dorset had just told the radio station that anybody who went out in this mess should have their head examined, when he took off in the patrol car at three miles an hour tops. At midnight Dorset found the farmhouse the woman described, but it was abandoned. "I knocked several times and shined my flashlight through the broken windows." Dorset got back in his car and headed down what he thought was the lane, but it wasn't. It was the ditch. The police radio was on the blink. He reached one guy on the CB and he said he wouldn't drive out in that weather for love nor money. Dorset stayed with his car and ate the bag of sugar cookies his sister gave him for the kids. They were shaped like Santa Claus. When the blizzard blew itself out about dawn, Dorset walked to the road and hitched a ride on the county plow. He said the incident restored his faith in humanity. "I was beginning to think nobody had a sense of humor anymore. People are great. That was a great joke, really."

 ## WINTER DRIVING

Survival Kit

No traveler should be without a winter survival kit. Keep it in the car at all times in case you are trapped in a blizzard. This is what I carry in my basic winter survival kit. It takes up most of the backseat, but peace of mind is worth it. Stay with your car until help or spring arrives, whichever comes first.

> *6 long-burning plumber's candles (for heat and cooking)*
>
> *kerosene stove and fuel cylinder (for extended stays)*
>
> *string*
>
> *extra blankets, sleeping bag*
>
> *dried foods*
>
> *5-gallon water jug, filled*
>
> *matches*
>
> *deck of cards*
>
> *flashlight, extra batteries*
>
> *transistor radio, extra batteries*
>
> *CB radio*

set of cooking utensils

wire

machete

rifle, extra shells

chain saw

toilet paper

paper towels

hunting bow, extra arrows

hunting knife

Bible

Hunting from a Stranded Car, *by Jack Jackson*

How to Field-Dress Game Inside a Car, *by Jack Jackson*

dot-to-dot puzzles

pictures of my family

first-aid kit

3 cartons of cigarettes for bartering

*twenty-foot fiberglass pole with red flag
(car locator)*

wash basin

soap

clean underwear

toothbrush, toothpaste

salt

ketchup

Starting the Car in Winter

If you drive to Minnesota in the winter and come from a place like Phoenix or Miami, where winter is when you turn off the air conditioner and open the windows, you could be in for a shock when you go outside your motel in the morning and try to start your car. It's one of the last great adventures in a world dominated by high tech.

Starting yourself when the temperature is minus 15 is hard enough, but starting your car is harder because it requires two people coordinating their efforts, one inside the car and one outside under the hood. And even that is no guarantee. In the rest of the country there's no such thing as a free lunch. We have a little free lunch all the time in Minnesota, but there's no such thing as a car that will start every time in the winter. And that would include the low-mileage rental car you drove from Arizona.

—"Hold it, hold it. We're not getting any juice. One of the jumper cables came off."

—"Are you sure you got negative connected to negative? There's smoke coming out of the radio."

—"Red is negative, isn't it?"

—"I thought black was negative. Try switching 'em."

—"Okay, there, got it. Hit that thing again."

—"It almost caught, it wanted to go."

—"Pump that footfeed. Kick it. Kick it. Don't flood it."

—"Maybe you should give it a shot of starting fluid. Not too much, though."

—"What? I couldn't hear you, I was squirting starting fluid in the carburetor throat. Hit it."

—"That was close. Shall I hit it again?"

—"Hold it a second. I'm gonna try pounding on the coil. Could be frozen coil. They'll do that. Okay, let's get serious now—before you turn the key, put your forehead on the steering wheel and lean into it, and think start—a lot of it's attitude. Hit it!"

—"Nothing."

—"Forget it. That's all she wrote."

At this point do what we do. Go back in and have a little lunch.

If you ever get your car started, then you're ready to plow into a snowdrift or skid off the road, in which case you need to know how to go about:

Getting the Car Out of the Snow When It's Stuck

As with starting the car, this procedure requires good communication skills.

Here's the deal. You bury your Buick in a large snowdrift on an unplowed street. At first you begin rocking the car by gunning it forward and then gunning it backward. Drop it into forward. Flip it into reverse. Forward. Reverse. If you are the person in the car, say nothing—you just grit your teeth and lunge. You can beat your forehead on the steering wheel, too, if you're in the dramatic mood. The person outside the car will stand back and encourage you:

—"You almost got it that time. Try it again."

—"That was close."

—"Gun it, gun it."

—"Stop, stop, something's hot under the car."

You probably hit Park instead of Reverse that last time. And with the wheels spinning at 80 miles an hour, that's hell on transmissions.

This is what Al—of Al's Transmission—will say. (Bob'll say it, too, and Ernie, and all the rest—forget shopping around.)

—"They don't give these transmissions away . . . I'd say we're talkin' six hundred bucks, and that's just to look at

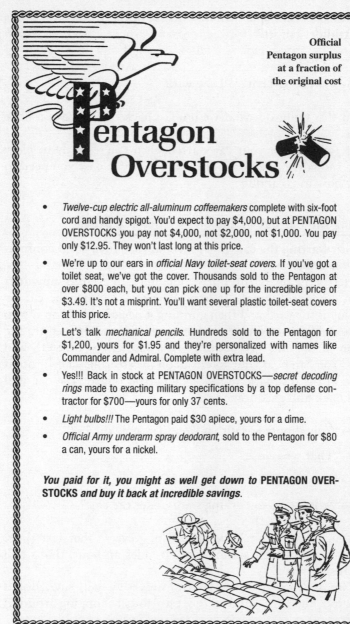

it . . . and if there's anything wrong with it, this is just a guesstimate, but, oh, I'd say somewhere around eight to nine hundred bucks . . . now that's if the bands are all okay, otherwise add three hundred. And if the housing is shot add another two hundred."

You can say

—"That seems like a lot for just a transmission."

But it won't do doodly squat for you. They've got you by the short hairs. Another thing: the bands are never okay.

What to Say When Someone Shows You His Smartphone

In 1987 the digitally challenged phone was what most of us had, so you can therefore be confident that the original lesson in connection with that antique device is still valid. Be advised that a landline rotary dial phone has "AARP" written all over it.

The following smartphone dialogue, like all the dialogues in classic *How to Talk Minnesotan*, is from an actual conversation, not from Wikipedia. The exchange is between Terry and Elmo, two old buddies for whom age forty is a fading memory. Purely by chance they ran into each other at the local medical clinic and are sitting side by side, waiting for the nurse to shout their first name loud enough to be heard in the parking lot.

TERRY: "Gotta tell you, Elmo, this smartphone is great! Look at this, look at this. See, you just touch it and—ahh, what happened!"

ELMO: "I think it shut off when you poked at it with your finger."

TERRY: "It's called touching, not poking."

ELMO: "Whatever, but it does look awkward."

TERRY: "Come on, Elmo, lighten up. Check this out. See, if I swipe the screen with my finger the photo I accidentally took this morning comes up. Cool, eh?"

ELMO: "You could say that. The photo seems to be a bare foot with a pretty decent dollop of Cool Whip on it."

TERRY: "Good call, Elmo. It is my foot. But that's not Cool Whip, it's a blob of shaving cream that fell off the razor when I was shaving."

ELMO: "Should a guy have his smartphone in the bathroom?"

TERRY: "I carry it with me wherever I go."

ELMO: "Would you answer the phone if you were in a public restroom?"

TERRY: "Why not?"

ELMO: "Hygiene and germs come to mind, as does the fact that a lotta guys know that a smartphone is also a camera."

TERRY: "I grant you that one, Elmo. But, listen, you gotta get one. You can see the actual weather on it by simply touching this little picture of a lightning bolt."

ELMO: "Yahbut, I can look outside to see what the weather is doing or go outside and stand in it to get a really good view."

TERRY: "Sure, Elmo, but can you see what the weather is in Idaho? One swipe left and I'm in Idaho."

ELMO: "I'm not interested in Idaho weather, not today anyway."

TERRY: "Wait a minute, wait a minute, some of the pictures are so danged tiny, hard to see, I'll put on my cheaters. Nope, it's not Idaho's weather radar. Sorry, it's my mobile bank account."

ELMO: "I hope it's not too mobile, Terry. Aren't you afraid there could be a privacy leak using the phone for banking?"

TERRY: "No, no, Elmo. I have the bank's privacy statement stored on my phone. Two taps and a swipe will get me to it."

ELMO: "No, I believe you do have it stored on your phone."

TERRY: "Here it is, no, sorry, that's an app that searches for restaurants in the area. I know the privacy statement is here someplace."

ELMO: "Maybe it's so private you can't find it."

TERRY: "This is no time for your sarcasm, Elmo. I'm just getting used to the phone."

ELMO: "I wonder if a guy should read the manual first."

TERRY: "You're talking Dark Ages, Elmo. This smartphone's operating system is all intuitive. There is no manual. What to do just comes to you, like wizardry."

ELMO: "My home phone doesn't have a manual either Terry, and the deal is when somebody calls me, it rings its bell, and I pick up the receiver and start talking, and I do it automatically."

TERRY: "I feel sorry for you, Elmo. You're gonna be left behind as the world surges into the future. And for your information we don't have mechanical bells on smartphones, we have ringtones. Mine plays 'The Times They Are A-Changin'' on bagpipes when a call comes in."

ELMO: "I'll take your word for it."

Books, Fuel Oil, and Coffee Crusades

Sadly Neglected Books from the Gopher State

An Overview for Visitors

by Marla R. Seemur, Historian

No matter where you live in the U.S., you've no doubt heard of (and maybe even read) *The Anderson Saga*, Knute Swenson's epic five-volume work that tells the story of one Minnesota family's rise to power in the dairy business. I'm not saying it's not a good book. Of course it is. "Two Hands, Four Teats," the chapter omitted in public-school editions of *Saga*, is the best writing of that kind I've seen. I do, however, agree with critics that "One Busy Bull," from Volume Two, has little to recommend it but the graphic humdrum of the barnyard. So, all things considered, a fairly good book, but it's not the only one. That's the point I want to make.

For a more balanced view of Minnesota, I'd like to suggest three books that deserve your attention. They'll be a wonderful preparation for your visit here.

Midgets in the Earth chronicles the struggles of a group of circus clowns to establish a home on the prairies in the mid-nineteenth century. This is probably the most sadly neglected book I have ever read.

Warm Quilts is the brutally realistic autobiographical account of Alma Moss's tragic lifelong fight against familial chilling.

Orville Remembers is one of the best oral histories ever compiled in Minnesota and that says a lot. Mike Budson has taken "the matter of Orville" and molded it into a series of finely crafted stories that deal with almost every aspect of life in Minnesota, including the past. I never get tired of reading in this huge book (1,568 tiny-print pages). I keep it beside my bed and often fall asleep with it in my hands. But why go on when I can show you its power? Here's one of my favorite stories from *Orville Remembers*.

"Nutmeg, I Think"
(from *Orville Remembers*)

I remember one time we had to go to town to buy somethin' at a store. I think it was sugar, but it might've been nutmeg. We drove to town in a car. We called 'em autos sometimes, too, which was short for automobile. These cars we drove had steering wheels. You maybe know what I mean. The steering wheel was round like a wheel and had spokes on a shaft. She connected to a kind of gearbox, so when you turned the steering wheel there in the driver's side of the auto or car, you see, that made the wheels in the front of the car turn different ways, depending on the way you turned the steering wheel. It was somethin', I'll tell you. You could go places and turn corners. She did the job, she really turned the car, that steering wheel. I guess I put in a lot of turning in my time, you bet.

We kept the keys to that car hangin' on a nail in the porch. A porch used to be this little room hooked on to a house. That porch of ours had shelves to put things on. They were something, the way they held things so they would be handy when you wanted 'em. You don't see shelves much anymore, not the kind we had. They made shelves to last in those days.

One time I was puttin' something up on one of those shelves. We did that back then. When we took something down, we put it back up there. It sure brings back memories. What was it I was puttin' up there that time? A pair of gloves, maybe, or it could've been a pliers. Anyway, just as I was reaching up there, I happened to look out the window we had there by the shelves and saw some clouds in the sky coming from the west. They were puffy and white, you know, and kept comin' over most of the day. Nowadays kids don't seem too interested in clouds.

It reminds me somehow of the time we had the Chevy on the road. Chevy was the name of our car. It was short for Chevrolet. Well, we came to a hill that went down to a creek. At the top of that hill we were doin' a good thirty miles an hour, but when we got to the bottom there by the bridge, we were doin' forty-five. A lot of times a car would do that, pick up speed goin' down a hill.

Funny how things come back to you. I remember the hog that ate slop like it was yesterday. Bought it from a neighbor. He was quite the character. Wore long underwear in the winter, you bet. He had a dog that would chase cars. I remember one time that dog of his barked at our Chevy when we had to go to town to buy somethin' at a store. Nutmeg, I think it was. But that's another story.

 # WHERE I LIVE AND WHAT I BURN FOR FUEL

[*Note*: The following story has appeared in several farm newspapers over the years. The author is anonymous and the names of the people and the town are obviously made up, but the story is true. The moral is clear: learning how to talk Minnesotan is hardly half the battle if you decide to make rural Minnesota your home. —H.M.]

When my wife and I moved to our farmhouse near Hornet, Minnesota, fourteen years ago, we needed number-one fuel oil for the furnace, so I called the Hornet Co-op Oil Station to order some up. It's the world's second co-op oil station, established just before the stock market crash in 1929, according to its sign. I never doubted it.

"This is Harold Mire," I said.

RURAL AUTHOR

I am twenty-four years old and because I wrote a book called *Growth*, about growing up in western Minnesota, I was invited to participate in a "new author" exposition at the U of M in 2009, where we would talk about our writing habits. The first author to speak was a very stylish dark-haired woman from New York City, who was chewing gum and sort of dancing around in her short skirt when she talked. What she read from her book was quite good, I thought, but pretty racy. She said she did all her writing at a desk near the open second-floor window in her Greenwich Village apartment. Her best work was done in the evenings, she said, as the local transvestites gathered below her window, talking and laughing and carrying on. Boy, she really got the applause from the crowd. I went up to the microphone and read a passage about bullhead fishing with my grandpa. I said I wrote my book in a very small room about 12 x 8 feet on the ground floor of an old farmhouse out on the prairies, and I had a window that faced north toward the grove of trees, and as far as I knew no transvestites had gathered outside. But deer walked by all the time, and I liked hearing off in the distance the Burlington Northern Santa Fe whistling for the crossings, two longs and one short, a peaceful sound that was always uplifting. Two or three people applauded, but mostly I think they were laughing at me. So I snuck out and got in my pickup and drove home.

—D.P., Granite Falls

"Harold *who*? Where do you live, anyway?"

I had that memorized. It's always a good idea to memorize where you live. "North of town," I said, "a long three miles on County Road 12. It's the farmplace on the hill."

"Hill?"

"Well, maybe it's more like a *rise*," I said, "or a large bump."

"County 12? Is that the blacktop that runs by the Methodist cemetery and takes a dogleg around the drainage ditch?"

"That's the one, only it takes another dogleg before it runs by us. We're right where the dog's paw would be."

The world's second co-op oil station seemed to lack a basic orientation, I thought, but I didn't mention it. Maybe the guy on the phone was new, too.

Then he said, "Oh, sure, you mean the Fletcher farm."

"I do?"

It turns out Orville Fletcher used to live where I live now. Orville had a habit of putting his initials into every concrete object he built during his long residency. The clean-out plug for the cement-block chimney says "O.F. '54." The steps to the cellar, "O.F. '37." The concrete floor in the dairy barn has a *row* of initials (Orville's brothers', probably), concluding with "O.F. '57." And a couple of cat tracks. Cats make good supervisors.

During my early fuel-ordering years in Hornet, I'd sometimes get an older fellow on the line. "This is Harold Mire. Could you please bring me some number-one fuel oil?" I would say.

"Who? Where?"

I knew the shortcut to my place by now. "Out at the Fletcher farm."

And he would say, "The *what*?"

"You know, two doglegs north on County 12, past the Methodist cemetery and along the ditch."

"Oh," he'd say, "you mean the Prindel place."

I've never been surprised by anything I've heard from the world's second co-op, so I said, "If the Prindel place is four acres of house and buildings with Orville Fletcher's initials all over everything, you got it."

It turns out the Prindels lived where I live before the Fletchers did. The Fletchers lived on the Prindel place, you see, and I live on the Fletcher farm. It seemed complicated, but I didn't question it. I kept hoping the Co-op would deliver the fuel oil to me and then bill it out to either Orville or one of the Prindels. But it was the other way around. I paid for the fuel oil and the Co-op delivered it to the Fletcher farm or the Prindel place, depending on who answered the phone. The Co-op didn't care where they delivered oil as long as I paid the bills.

My wife and I moved to the country because we wanted to live the life we read about in *Little House on the Prairie* and *Bambi*. But living in somebody else's house on their land and paying for their fuel oil made it pretty hard to smell the flowers and become one with nature. It was even getting difficult to become one with ourselves.

But we knew that if anything happened in a small town it happened very slowly or not at all.

About six or seven years ago I called the Co-op to order some number-one fuel oil, identifying myself by name, which was still Harold Mire, although I developed a nervous tic whenever I said it.

"This is Harold Mire. I need some number-one fuel oil."

"You bet," the guy at the Co-op said.

You bet. I suppose I should have put it in the local news section of the *Hornet Eagle*. "The Harold Mire family of rural Hornet recently began ordering fuel oil under their own name."

A couple of years ago when I examined the deed and title to the Mire bump, I found out the Fletchers and the Prindels were interlopers like me, and it made me feel a little better. The St. Peter Railroad owned it before them, and the state of Minnesota before that, and the United States government before that. It wasn't mentioned in the title, but of course the U.S. government got the place from France. France, I assume, got it from the Sioux Indians, but I don't think they worked through a realtor.

It's probably our destiny to stay where we are—you know where, two doglegs north past the Methodist cemetery on County 12. But if we ever do have to sell the Mire bump and move away, I hope the new owners aren't strangers coming to the country to find out who they are in the large scheme of things. They'll be lucky if the world's second co-op oil station finds out who they are.

B—U—D—G—E—T
EXERCISE SYSTEM

Why spend $500 for a bunch of heavy weights when all you need is BUDGET CARGO STRAPS. Easily attached to ordinary household furnishings. Start by carrying light objects, like the kitchen table or the clothes hamper, and slowly work your way up to the refrigerator and the washing machine. In a year you'll have a piano on your back and people will hardly know you.

Why pay thousands of dollars for treadmills and trampolines, when all you need is BUDGET VELCRO EXERCISE SHOES, the sport shoe with Velcro soles. Just fifteen minutes a day of walking on your living room carpet with Budget Velcro shoes and you'll be a lot thinner, and so will your carpet.

Also from Budget Exercise, back in stock by popular demand, the BUDGET FALLING MACHINE. Scientific studies have shown that when you slip and fall every muscle in your body is exercised, some you didn't even know you had. The Budget Falling Machine simulates nature's most perfect exercise. With five fall levels, including Trip and Flail, Loose Rug, and Head over Heels. Simply fasten yourself to the Budget Falling Machine with the grappling hooks, set the level, and you can fall over and over again without hurting yourself all that much. But you'll feel it for days.

BUDGET HOME EXERCISE SYSTEM
Sweating will never be cheaper.
Some assembly required.

Minnesota Lutheran Church Coffee Crusades: An Update

Twenty-five years ago the Lutherans were strong in Minnesota, and the parishioners were a good source for talking Minnesotan and remain so to this day. Back in 1987, when the *Star Tribune* interviewed me about *How to Talk Minnesotan*, I suggested that in addition to using the visitor's guide, out-of-state visitors could pick a Lutheran church and participate as best they could, going to basement suppers, playing basketball on sports night, signing up for the canoe retreat in the north country (men only) or the quilting group (women only), and as a last resort listen to the sermon. Minnesota's Lutheran pastors are trained in Greek and Hebrew, but their first language is Minnesotan. Luther Seminary in St. Paul, Minnesota, has a special course in Minnesotan for pastors from other states who wish to be called to a Lutheran church in Minnesota; otherwise, they would not have a prayer.

In 1987 church basement coffee (CBC) was served at wedding receptions, at funeral lunches, and during the various church festivals. Church basement coffee was a staple, and easily identified. When one was served a cup of coffee in a Lutheran church, for it to be true CBC, one needed to see the bottom of the cup clearly through the lightly colored liquid. Few parishioners ever get the jitters from church basement coffee.

In greater Minnesota, which means rural, most Lutheran churches stick to tradition and serve CBC only at church events, including upstairs before the church service with doughnut holes and selected bars. In 2003 Gary (not his real name) was assigned coffee duties for Sunday morning at a Lutheran church in a southwestern Minnesota village and thought maybe a guy should give everybody a treat. He bought two pounds of Caribou's Colombian Full City Roast and dumped it into the big V-2 rocket–shaped aluminum percolator. "There's something wrong with this coffee" was whispered around the fellowship room so as not to hurt Gary's feelings. Gary heard some of the men, even a deacon, making references to crankcase oil and other petrochemicals.

But I would be remiss if I did not talk about the unfortunate conflict among Lutherans that erupted slowly beginning about 2006, though some say there were signs of discontent as far back as 2002 in the larger parishes of the Twin Cities. The media referred to it as the "Coffee Wars." In 2008 YouTube went nuts on it, and lots of very fine parishioners were made to look like dopes, which seems to be the primary purpose of YouTube. The "Coffee Wars" were all over Facebook, where friends became frenemies over a cup of coffee. Trouble was brewing.

The shot heard round the Twin Cities area came from Church X when it installed a streaming digitized outdoor sign that announced times for services and sermon titles. It was not long before X's streaming sign began providing time and temperature, a practical addition from the newly hired IT pastor. Some parishioners, living as they did in the Twin Cities, and quite accustomed to a solid cup of coffee from Starbucks, began asking for better coffee during the preservice fellowship. Starbucks provided Church X with pump containers and two Sunday morning blends. The IT pastor streamed "Starbucks served here, today's blend, Waker Upper."

A parishioner and his wife on their way to Church Y saw the sign, slowed down, looked at each other, and whipped into X's lot. They were welcomed with open arms and a good cup of Waker Upper, room for cream, no sugar. The couple later notified their pastor at Church Y that they were thinking about changing their membership.

I don't wish to take sides, though I will say that when Church X started streaming the Minnesota Lottery numbers for the Saturday drawing, it seemed a bit on the tacky side. But who am I to judge.

This conflict made its rounds on Facebook and e-mail. Google "Coffee Wars" if you have a strong stomach.

It was not long until many churches upped the ante and began offering mochas, lattes, and espresso for Sunday fellowship, trying to outdo each other, which, pardon me, does seem a trifle inappropriate.

During the highly competitive Advent season in 2011, Lutheran Church R advertised cappuccino and maple scones on their Web page. Parishioners from Church Z, Church J, and several couples from the Presbyterian Church around the corner showed up. But they didn't stay for the sermon.

Lesson 14

Doctors and Patients in Minnesota

 VISITING THE DOCTOR

The following is an actual conversation between a Minnesota doctor and a Minnesota patient, recorded by hidden microphones in the examining room. Nothing has been deleted. What's to hide?

DOCTOR: "So, how're you feeling then?"

PATIENT: "Oh, not too bad, really, Doc. I hate to bother you."

D: "No problem. Any discomfort?"

P: "Oh, yeah, a little. Nothing to get excited about, I don't think. I was down in this area anyway, so I thought I'd check with you, just in case it's something. But if you're busy, I could always come back. It's not like it's a big deal."

D: "You don't look all that bad, professionally speaking."

P: "It could be worse. I can live with it. What do you think it could be?"

D: "It could be anything."

P: "That's kinda what I thought, too."

D: "On the other hand, it could be what's going around. I been seeing a lot of that lately. Let me feel your forehead."

P: "Have I got a fever?"

D: "She's a little warm, but then my hand's cold. Have you been taking any medication?"

P: "Dry toast is all."

D: "Would you say you're worse than you were or better?"

P: "Better, today, I'd say."

D: "Well, then, just keep doing whatever it is you're doing to get better."

P: "I haven't been doing too much at all, really. Mostly lying on the davenport watching TV."

D: "Sounds good to me. Anything else I can help you with then?"

P: "No, Doc, that should do her. I thought, well, better safe than sorry. Should I come back in a week or so to see how I'm doing then?"

D: "Whatever. You know how you feel better than I do."

NORTHWOODS HMO

NORTHWOODS HMO is the industry leader in minimal care for the lowest possible cost. Ask about our heart pacer* special, two for the price of one, installation not included.

The following interview with a NORTHWOODS HMO customer says it all. The reporter is not an employee of NORTHWOODS HMO. Mr. Olson was not paid to participate in the interview.

REPORTER: Mr. Olson, first of all, is NORTHWOODS HMO your health care provider?

OLSON: Yep.

REPORTER: Have you been pretty happy with NORTHWOODS HMO then?

OLSON: You bet.

REPORTER: When did you sign up with NORTHWOODS HMO?

OLSON: Right after they renovated the old school building and hung up their shingle on the door.

REPORTER: When was that then?

OLSON: It was the year I raised up and hit my head on the oak dining room table looking for my hearing aid.

REPORTER: Did NORTHWOODS HMO treat your injury?

OLSON: I wasn't signed up with them yet. It was only a concussion anyway, at least that's what my wife said it was, because I couldn't remember her name for over a year.

REPORTER: I suppose after you signed on with NORTHWOODS HMO the staff helped with your recovery from the concussion.

OLSON: Nope. They said the bonk on the head was a preexisting injury and none of their business.

REPORTER: Would you recommend NORTHWOODS HMO as a superior health care facility?

OLSON: Well, I wouldn't go that far, I guess, but it's okay, though.

REPORTER: Strong words from a satisfied NORTHWOODS HMO customer.

*Refurbished to almost the original specs in our labs

TWO COMMON MINNESOTA DISEASES

Chances are if you get anything while you're in Minnesota you'll get *what's going around*. It's epidemic most of the year. Ninety-five percent of the people who call in sick to work have *what's going around*.

—"I can't make it to work today. I could barely get out of bed to drink liquids. I don't have any energy. I'm pretty sure it's *what's going around*."

What's going around is often brought on by going outside with wet hair and getting chilled. If you suspect you have *what's going around*, you're probably right, but if you want a second opinion, have somebody's mother feel your forehead.

If it's not *what's going around*, it could be *Hotdish Revenge*. *Hotdish Revenge* is caused by eating warmed-up hotdish on the third day. Something about hotdish makes it a playground for microbes after a while. If you don't know how long it's been in the refrigerator, you'd better feed it to the cats. Cats are immune to hotdish that's over the hill.

—"Do you want to go drive around the Metrodome and see if it's still inflated for the Vikings game?"

—"Boy, it's tempting—that Metrodome is so beautiful—and I got over *what's going around*—but now I think I've got a case of *Hotdish Revenge*. I'm gonna stay in the house and do a little light trotting from room to room."

A few hints for non-Minnesotans thinking about practicing medicine in Minnesota:

1. If you went to an out-of-state medical school, just clean instruments and recorded music won't do the trick for you. Unless you study Minnesotans and their language, you could be the one out there in your waiting room all day reading old magazines and listening for your name to be called.

2. Don't talk too much. Nothing scares a Minnesotan more than a doctor who rattles on and on, and that includes saying too much about what you're doing to the patients or for them.

3. Minnesotans figure it's less trouble all the way around if they never get sick. This can have an economic impact on those in the health-care-delivery field.

    You see, our aim in life is to have nothing wrong with us when we buy the farm. Jogging probably helps toward that end. That's why we jog here. We don't experience the highs from running claimed in other states (it's mostly lows) and we don't have any illusions that running down a road every day will necessarily make us live longer than anybody else. But it might keep us healthy until we die.

    Take the newspaper story of one Minnesota jogger's last run. He was putting his miles in on a gravel road—the same road he had used for nearly twenty years—and although there weren't any witnesses, the evidence indicates that his number was up: his body stopped and he just pitched forward, skidded a little on his right shoulder and lay there dead until his neighbor drove by and slung him in the back of his pickup and drove him home. He was the picture of health when he died. He should have been proud of himself.

4. We do get sick in Minnesota, but we pretend that we aren't sick until our symptoms are unmistakable. In some ways this makes the practice of medicine easier in Minnesota: anybody could diagnose what's wrong by the time most of us make an appointment. On the other hand, if we know what's wrong, why go to the doctor?

GET-WELL CARDS

The quilted cards with flowers and cheerful messages in rhyme are fine for people in other states. But here we prefer something a little less direct. When I was in the hospital for some tests—they thought it was gonna be my gallbladder, but it turned out to be nothing, which is what I figured—I got a cheerful card from

my brother: it had a picture of a John Deere combine on the front going through wheat. Inside was a picture of a loaf of bread. My brother added a personal message: "We got about 4/10ths last night." I appreciated the sentiments.

 # WHERE TO GO IN MINNESOTA

Pageants

[*Note*: Going to a lake and fishing is the most popular tourist activity in Minnesota. Going to a lake and thinking about fishing while you sit in the shade in front of the cabin and drink beer is the second most popular tourist activity. They're both hard to beat. What's in third place is a toss-up, depending on who you talk to. For my money, it's Minnesota's pageants. Myself, I got the pageant bug when I used to watch the Macy's Thanksgiving Day parade on TV with my grandpa. Every time I see a large figure blown up with gas, I think of him. That's why I consider myself lucky to live in Minnesota—we've got pageantry coming out our ears. It's an institution here. I asked M. Sam Johnson, director of the Minnesota Pageant Council, if he wouldn't write a few words about Minnesota's rich tradition of pageantry. —H.M.]

> Dear Harold:
>
> Glad to take time out from my busy schedule and help you beef up your book. I'm always happy to talk about pageants, as you know. When I replaced Rick Borg at the helm of the Minnesota Pageant Council (after Rick was appointed Peat Moss Development Officer by the governor) I knew that the pageantry industry was burgeoning and I felt very strongly that pageants would someday rival Minnesota's lakes in vacation clout. So when an independent study placed Minnesota number one in pageantry among the fifty states this year, I was gratified. A personal goal for next year is to get

"Pageant Capital of the Western Hemisphere" on our license plates. The flying loon and the pocket gopher with its head sticking out of a hole don't do us justice.

There are 793 pageants currently registered with the Pageant Council and 300-plus others actively seeking our endorsement. A pageant qualifies for certification if it achieves thirty-two spectacle units on its maiden outing. The MPC spectacle team evaluates it in the areas of concept, costuming, music, gross revenue, scene design, parade, coronation, impact, and overall sincerity. If a pageant has followed our guidelines but still falls short of the thirty-two-point target, we send a task force out.

A case in point was the Composting Pageant in Borstarck. Borstarck, as you know, has since put itself on the map with their pageant, but the first year it looked like a loser and received only sixteen spectacle units. But we thought it had potential. So I assigned Gordon Pinto—our best troubleshooter—to the Borstarck job. Gordy, as you maybe recall, got a lot of press attention when he singlehandedly turned Garsinia's Corn Cob Days around. Gordy saw immediately that the problem with the Composting Pageant was 95 percent conceptual. It's a damn good three-star pageant now.

But I won't pretend it's all been a bed of roses, Harold. I refer to Swipton's so-called Wet T-Shirt Pageant. The town council and the American Legion in Swipton went through proper channels with their Sugar Beet Pageant. It was certified with a four-star rating. It was a fine, family-oriented pageant, with barbershop quartets, a beet opera, and the "endless procession of beets." Something or somebody must've snapped up there, because we started getting letters from shocked and disappointed travelers who said if they wanted that kind of disgusting entertainment they'd stay home and watch cable TV. There's no telling how many tourists we lost to Wisconsin and South Dakota over that pageant. We censured Swipton immediately and finally had no choice but to withdraw certification when they refused to clean up their act. We can play hardball when we have to.

Maybe this isn't the place to mention it, but another thorn in my side was the Poetry Pageant in Sedgely. I knew exactly where that one went wrong, and I righted it. When I began getting complaints from tourists that the poetry didn't sound like poetry, it sounded like newspaper articles, I went out to Sedgely. I could not believe what I found. Most of the "poems" they had been foisting on the crowds were indeed prose. I showed the incriminating evidence to the Poetry Pageant president and he said those were *prose poems.* That's what he said, *prose poems.* I laughed in his face and informed him that poetry rhymed and had lines of a certain length and went *da-dum, da-dum, de-de-da, da-dum,* and so forth, and anybody with a third-grade education knew that.

But enough of the negative. I'm going to let you in on something, but I have to ask you not to use it in your book. The MPC is working on a major pageant of its own that will celebrate the subject of Minnesota pageantry itself. It will be a superb entertainment vehicle, but also educational. We expect it to raise pageant consciousness tremendously. We're pretty darned excited about it.

Well, Harold, I hope this is what you wanted, or close. Drop by MPC headquarters sometime when you're in town. I slipped in a copy of our latest guide for you. Feel free to reprint anything you want from it.

Vive la Pageants,
M. Sam Johnson

Selections from *Pageants Galore!!*—the official MPC guide to Minnesota Pageants:

✓ Exposed-Rock Pageant

Hardstone, Minnesota, June 2. First pageant certified by the MPC, first to receive five-star rating. The enormous slabs of granite dotting the landscape around Hardstone were only stumbling blocks to the early settlers, who had no suspicion they were dynamiting full basements out of the world's oldest exposed rock, as later determined by a team of scientists. The Exposed-Rock Pageant is the exuberant celebration of this geological fact.

The carnival of delights includes the lively acrobatics of the Wizard of Stone (Hardstone's mayor), the hilarious mock-rock auction, and the dancing Shetlands. Some travelers to Minnesota are said to return each year for the tasty Nugget Dogs alone, a patented novelty food of hot dog chunks wrapped in lefse and deep-fat fried to look like tiny boulders.

✓ Running-Water Pageant

Bellabeut, August 23. A spectacle of the first order, this pageant commemorates the construction of the new water tower in 1971 and again in 1972. (The footings for the legs weren't deep enough on the first one and it tipped over during a blizzard on a Sunday in December of '72. It crushed the municipal liquor store and knocked the bank off its foundation and washed the drive-in facility down the street almost to the railroad tracks. But nobody was hurt.) The pageant starts at dawn and features twenty pumper trucks and 5,000 feet of fire hose. Good local acting and plenty of laughs. Bring a raincoat and a change of clothes.

✓ Duel of the Giants

Last Sunday in August, at the Carl Bintoton farm, two miles south and a mile east of Trasto, or six miles west and a mile north of Wadden. Called the "Battle of the Red and Green," each year a late-model International tractor (Red) is matched with a late-model John Deere tractor (Green) of the same horse-power and the drivers go at each other until one of the tractors is just a pile of parts and an oil slick. Very popular. The outcome has a significant effect on farm equipment purchases in the Midwest. Noisy but funny. Pork feed on the grounds. Parade. Queen.

✓ *Particle Board Pageant*

June 14, Millborton. A small, carefully crafted dramatization of the impact of the compressed-wood-chip industry on the town's economy. Those of you in the market for wall paneling can buy it at 30 percent off on pageant day. Delivery is extra.

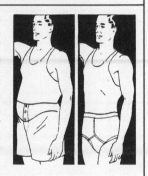

Lesson 15

Talking Money and Road Repairs in Minnesota

 **INDIRECTNESS**

Being too direct in Minnesota is a common mistake made by visitors. For example, if you're not from around here, and you drive into a gas station, you might be tempted to say

—"Fill it with lead-free, check the oil, and get the windshield."

A Few of the Phrases of Indirection Out of Thousands

✓ *If you feel like it*
✓ *If it's not too much trouble*
✓ *If a guy*
✓ *A lotta guys*

These and many other Minnesota words and phrases are used to make indirect commands and statements. Let's head back to the gas station and listen to a Minnesotan talking to the attendant.

—"Yeah, I'll take a little lead-free then, and you could maybe check the oil if you go past the hood, if it's not too much trouble. Whatever. No big rush. I'll do the windshield. I have to get out and check the tires anyway, you know."

Two people approach the reference desk at the public library. Which one is the Minnesotan?

A: "I want a book on mountain goats."

B: "If you're not too busy, ma'am, I was sort of wondering if you could maybe help me find a book about mountain goats then?"

The driver of a car has parked with the back end out in heavy traffic. Which speaker is the Minnesotan?

A: "Say, Mert, you could maybe move in a little closer to the curb if you wanted to then."

B: "Mert, move this pile of junk before we get our butts knocked off."

✓ A Lotta Guys, A Guy Could

Another common Minnesota phrase of indirection is a *guy could* and its variations, including *if a guy* and *a lotta guys*. Here's a Minnesotan who's been asked about how to repair a leaking toilet:

—"Well, I think if a guy took off that float valve with a Vise Grips, he could maybe get at the gasket then."

See how different that is from:

—"Take off the float valve, dummy!"

Again:

—"I wonder if a guy couldn't attach a handle to that thing without too much trouble."

At the smelt feed:

—"A guy could sit here all night and eat smelt and beans."

A lotta guys do, too—as long as the beer holds out.

A lotta guys is often used to give an opinion when it was not asked for but is maybe needed anyway.

—"A lotta guys wouldn't use a welder so close to a gas tank like that."

A lotta guys is also used in sarcastic statements. If a stud wall on a house under construction has just fallen over, a Minnesotan might say to his carpenter friend:

—"A lotta guys would've braced that wall, Joe."

Recognizing Minnesota sarcasm is one of the toughest lessons a visitor can learn. A lotta guys never hear the difference.

A lotta guys and its variations are used mostly by Minnesota men, but not exclusively. The phrase *a lotta gals* should never be substituted for *a lotta guys*. If the friend helping fix the toilet is a woman, a guy should know better than to say:

—"I think if a gal took off that float valve with a Vise Grips, she could maybe get at the gasket then."

Her natural reply would be:

—"I wonder if a guy could talk with a Vise Grips clamped on his nose?"

On a first date, a Minnesota man might easily say:

—"Do you suppose a guy could maybe get a kiss before you went inside?"

The Minnesota woman could say:

—"A lotta guys wouldn't ask."

Or she could say:

—"If a guy left right now he could be a block away before I got sick."

Minnesota women are not as indirect as Minnesota men.

TALKING MONEY

Phrases

✓ *How much do I owe you?*
✓ *Let's settle up.*
✓ *Your money's no good here.*
✓ *What's this?*

Some Minnesota Proverbs to Keep in Mind

Money talks, but not much.

Every good turn deserves to be paid back.

A gift out of the blue is like a kick in the teeth.

You don't compliment me, I won't criticize you.

It is better to give—receiving is not a good deal.

As long as you don't make friends during your visit here, you'll be okay when it comes to money. But if you stay awhile, trouble could develop. The following dialogue between two neighbors in Minnesota is word-for-word as it occurred. If you think you understand it completely, write me a letter—I know it's right, I just don't understand why.

—"Boy, Harold, my car works real good after you fixed the carburetor. Thanks."

—"You bet. No problem."

—"How much do I owe you?"

—"Owe me? Not a dime. Your money's no good, so stop talking."

—"But I want to settle up with you. You must've worked an hour out there in the cold."

—"I worked two and a half hours out there in the cold, Arnie, but I'm not gonna take your money, so forget it."

—"Sheez, Harold, I feel bad—let me give you something for your trouble. Here, take this twenty, it's the least I can do."

—"No, it's not the least you can do—you can take that twenty and put it back in your billfold. Don't get me mad."

—"Look, Harold, I'm gonna lay this twenty on the table here, and then I'm gonna walk away. What you do is up to you."

—"What I'm doin' is, Arnie, I'm picking this twenty up and stuffing it in your shirt pocket, and if you take it out again and wave it in my direction, *I'm* gonna walk away."

—"You haven't heard the last of this, Harold. I'm gonna figure out some way to pay you back."

—"Whatever."

 # WHERE TO GO IN MINNESOTA

Minnesota Academy of Handypersons Award Ceremony

—by Lester Brown, acting chairperson of the Academy

If you're here the first Saturday in February, there's something you shouldn't miss. I'm talking about the gala handypersons event of the year, when the Minnesota Academy of Handypersons gives the cherished Golden Vise Grips to the top handymen and handywomen of Minnesota.

Television coverage begins as the guests and nominees from all over Minnesota begin arriving in their vans and pickups at the curb outside the old Dell Theatre in St. Paul. You see a lot of toolboxes, and hammers hanging from belt loops, pliers in leather holsters, steeltoed shoes, overalls, flannel shirts.

The ceremony officially opens when the lights dim and the grand old man of Handypersons, John "Shingles" Lister, shouts the rallying words of the Academy: "Say, I can fix that. Let me get my tools!!" John—regarded as the "best damned roofer in the business, bar none"—is joined as always by the beautiful co-hostess, Doris Peterson, the first woman ever to be inducted into the Home Repair Hall of Fame. They say she was born with a three-eighths variable-speed reversible drill in her hand.

From then on it's pandemonium as the nominations are made in each category and the Golden Grippies presented to the winners.

For information about tickets and a colorful booklet with biographical information about past winners, write to the Minnesota Academy of Handypersons.

What follows is a list of some of this year's nominees and winners. (An asterisk denotes the winner.)

✓ Best Handy Idea

Nominees:

Teddy Nichols (extending the life of egg cartons with varnish)

Irene Field (spice shelf organization plan)

*Bud Bowman (patching old overshoes)

✓ Most Amazing Single Handy Act

Nominees:

*Ephra Glenwood (repairing and replacing the ball-valve float assembly in a toilet tank without shutting off the water) [Ephra told the audience his secret was long rubber gloves and making sure your tools are greased.]

Mike Mikelson (reducing refrigerator odor with a simple device made from a food blender and two feet of garden hose)

Leo Rossburger (jump-starting his car in a blizzard with static electricity from his wife's raccoon coat)

✓ *Creative Recycling*

Nominees:

Andy Richmond (studio couch made from chunks of truck tires found along the highway)

DeeDee Whalen (revolving doghouse made from a discarded washing machine)

*Henry H. Holtrow (typewriter paper from old clothes)

✓ *Best Handy Group Performance*

Nominees:

Bob, Bart, and Bernie Bogen (group insulation)

Roger and Edna Abbott and son Gordy (group carpeting)

*The Flying Sheetrockers (four neighbors from Ortonville) [The Flying Sheetrockers stole the show this year when they demonstrated their art on a bare 8-by-24-foot wall. They measured, cut, and installed all the Sheetrock in less than three minutes.]

TALKING ROAD REPAIRS

This is a primer of road-repair talk transcribed from an actual conversation, and used with permission. This is the first ten minutes. The full conversation is available by request.

—"What are they doing out there on 45?"

—"They're gonna widen it."

—"I thought it looked like they were moving the telephone lines back a ways."

—"It's gonna be kinda tough for detours, see, 'cause 45 right now is the way around the bridges they're putting in on 72."

—"Typical."

—"The one bridge they just replaced last year, and here they are tearing it down to put in another one."

—"I took that road last week. It looks like they're putting in seven, eight, I don't know, nine bridges."

—"They're tearing out nine bridges, but they're gonna put culverts in five of them. They say some of them don't need a bridge, really, because the creek was rerouted last year. But we'll see."

—"Oh, the new dam. Right."

—"It's gonna be tough getting to town. I figure it's about twenty-five miles farther now."

—"You got that right. Twenty-five hard miles. That gravel road is not the best either that goes off west there past the old Martinson place."

—"That has got to be the worst excuse for a road I have ever seen. And then they go and use it for the detour."

—"It's like driving on railroad ties."

—"If they'd come out here and asked us we coulda told them to route the traffic over that wide township road south there. You know the one I mean."

—"I know. The slough road. It was overbuilt at the time. Looks like a freeway. Nobody ever on it."

—"It was supposed to be blacktopped in '79 or '80, but all they got done was the grading. That's the one I take."

—"When they figure they'll be done with all this?"

—"When they figure or when they'll be done? They say by Labor Day. But I don't know."

—"Maybe Labor Day next year."

—"That would be more like it. I remember that piece of County 8 they resurfaced in 1974. What was it, all of ten miles? They had that thing tore up from March till Thanksgiving."

—"Wasn't that because the ground was so soft?"

—"That's what they said, but that road was there for who knows how long. Did it get soft while they were working on it, or what?"

Romance and Marriage: An Update

The Romance and Marriage lesson of 1987 is still pretty much valid, according to a survey conducted in 2002 by an independent organization hired by the state of Minnesota. But that said, a couple of changes should be noted in our rather active courtship and marriage activities in the Gopher State since 1987.

In 2012 courting in Minnesota by e-mail, by Facebook, and even (though rather rare) by Twitter has a particular fascination for Minnesota men especially, because not one of these media has direct physical contact as a factor in finding a potential love of one's life, and heck, that sure saves a lot of trouble of the kind you can imagine if you had to be there right in person and think of something to say, or be expected to hug or something, or go to a fancy restaurant.

It is important to note that Minnesota dating, courtship, and marriage took a hard right turn in 1983, when the Domestic Claims Court of Minnesota ruled in favor of the wife who sued her husband for more hugs, thus creating a great burden to many Minnesota men. The plaintiff, arguing her own case, proved beyond a shadow of doubt that her husband never initiated any hugs, and when she hugged him, he drew back and screwed up his face like somebody in pain.

In 2007 the Domestic Appellate Court heard an appeal by three Minnesota husbands representing the class of Minnesota Husbands made on the grounds that it violates a Minnesota man's constitutional right to be unemotional, if he feels like it. The appeal was denied and the three plaintiffs were the object of several humorous editorial cartoons and no end of comments at work.

I want to strongly point out that I tried to remain neutral on the ruling and the appeal, but neutral left me sleeping in the basement on the sofa bed with the iron bar under the mattress that digs into a guy's back, so I bit the bullet, took a side, and then there was no more talk of separate vacations.

But strangely, independent of the ruling, Minnesota men began showing signs of growing affectionate behavior in regard to their wives in the area of hugs. Experts believe it started, another surprise, with men holding hands with their wives. One thing can lead to another, as we know. That's not to say it's an epidemic yet, but I'm telling you that it's quite the deal to see Minnesota men hugging their wives in public, mostly the one-arm side hug, but there's also been a huge jump in the full-frontal hug, with the concomitant patting of the recipient's back, in private or right out in the open where somebody might see you.

Social scientists at the University of Minnesota are baffled by this outbreak, but university climatologists are not. There is convincing evidence that the increased frequency of husbands hugging their wives coincides with global warming. It is predicted that at the present rate of warming, marital hugging could go viral about the time the Atlantic Ocean begins seriously nibbling at Manhattan's real estate.

This is all good news for wives, but before somebody thinks of awarding a Nobel Prize to Minnesota men, it must be said that Minnesota men remain semi-adamant about hugging relatives or friends, male or female. They'll do it, but it is not a pretty sight.

Romance and Marriage in Minnesota

Minnesotan is not high on the list of the world's romance languages, but it's not quite as bad as some people make out. We do just fine here with dating and all the rest. I've got no complaints. But the fact is, if you're taking a vacation for romance, you'd be better off in Hawaii or Ohio. They pay the price for that reputation though. But you never know, you could meet that special person right here in Minnesota. Many of us have.

DATING

—"So you don't have to, Cindy, but I was wondering if you might want to go someplace with me, not tonight exactly, but you know, sometime then?"

—"Well, I could think of a lot worse things, David."

—"So, Friday then?"

—"No problem, David, it might even be fun."

You may quite possibly be very excited about your first date, but it's best to suppress that excitement. Don't go out of control. My experience is that it could turn out different from what you might expect, and so why stick your neck out and get your hopes up and then have them dashed. It's better to keep your hopes down to a realistic level, or even lower.

But, even in Minnesota you can be caught by surprise and the sparks will fly. One minute you're just drifting along, and the next minute, there you are, in the middle of a passionate romance. The following romantic encounters did happen in Minnesota, but what I wouldn't like to say is how I got the information. Let's just leave it that they're true, and I have my sources. And don't jump to conclusions about my private life either. Some of these encounters may have involved me and maybe not. I'm not real big on intimate confessions. Actually I'm not big on confessions period.

FALLING HEAD OVER HEELS IN MINNESOTA

At the Laundromat

—"I dropped my quarters all over the place, ma'am. I must've tripped on the bedspread hanging out of my clothes basket."

—"You should have a belt-loop change holder like mine. They sell them at Ben Franklin. They're real handy."

—"What a great idea. This is all so new to me."

—"That's what I figured. It's written all over your face. I'm Edna, by the way—and you dropped your Wisk."

—"Thanks. Wally here. Would I be out of line if I asked you something? It's personal."

—"I don't mind if you get personal."

—"What temperature setting should I use on the dryer?"

—"Use the warm setting for polyesters, but for everything else I turn it all the way up to high. Except underwear."

—"What's the deal on underwear, anyway?"

—"High heat wrecks the elastic in the waistband."

—"You sure know your way around, don't you? I hate baggy underwear."

—"So do I, Wally. Maybe it's a sign."

At the Garden Center

—"I didn't mean to brush my sweaty arm against your shoulder. I was reaching for a packet of Wacko Wonder pole beans. My name is Tom."

—"Don't apologize, Tom, it was wonderful. I'm Nina, and I like your taste in string beans—that Wacko Wonder is a good producer."

—"You got that right, but they're a little tough late in the season."

—"That's the way it goes, we can't have everything. When the long brown hairs on your arm touched my bare shoulder, I was reaching for the Giant Hybrid Radish."

—"Boy, good choice. What's your carrot?"

—"The Orange Blimp. But they get woody if the weather is dry and hot."

—"That's what I've heard, but they say it's a good keeper."

—"It's hard to find a good keeper, isn't it, Tom?"

—"You know, Nina, I want to say something, but I'm real nervous. It'll probably sound totally ridiculous and you'll laugh in my face. And I don't want you to think I just go around saying stuff like this all the time."

—"Spit it out, Tom."

—"I was wondering if maybe you and I could find a plot of rich earth and plant a garden together."

—"Oh, Tom, I can see us now on our hands and knees, weeding the rutabagas, the edible-pod peas, and the okra."

—"I don't like okra."

—"We can work it out."

At the Hardware Store

—"Yikes!"

—"Did you feel it too? A spark jumped between us."

—"You want to know what I think?"

—"Do I have a choice?"

—"That spark was caused by static electricity. It means there was a potential difference built up between us, and when we got close, electrons were transferred at the speed of light, leaving us electrically neutral relative to each other."

—"I haven't exactly been waiting all my life for somebody to say that to me, but it's better than nothing."

—"I was a little afraid, but I'm glad I let it out, ma'am."

—"What do you say we walk around and build up some more static charges and then release them?"

In the Parking Lot of a Shopping Mall, Winter

—"So you've got your hood up then, ma'am."

—"The engine goes around and around when I turn the key, but it won't start, and I smell gas."

—"Can I be frank?"

—"Do it. Time is running out."

—"My guess is your automatic choke is stuck shut. See, the deal is, if that choke flap sticks down, then the engine can't get any air through the carburetor throat, and it floods."

—"Is there anything you can do for me?"

—"You bet. I'm gonna take your air cleaner off and loosen up your choke flap."

—"Can I help?"

—"Yeah, sure. You can get behind the wheel then and crank her over, but your battery is pretty weak so I gotta move my Chevy up real close and hook up the jumper cables."

—"Jumper cables? I've lived in Minnesota all my life and this is the first time anybody has jumped me. I suppose you're an old hand at it?"

—"I can do it with my eyes closed, ma'am."

—"Let's both keep our eyes open on this one, okay?"

On the Dock of One of Minnesota's Ten or Fifteen Thousand Lakes

—"I'm sorry, what a klutz. I snagged your line with that last cast."

—"Don't worry about it, ma'am, it's the only action I've had all day. Fishing is just not my strong suit."

—"My bobber's tangled in your hook. Let me cut the whole thing off and give you a new setup out of my tackle box."

—"No problem, ma'am."

—"Your sinker's too heavy, did you know that?"

—"Where have you been all my life?"

—"Well, for one thing, I don't usually fish this lake. Could I make a suggestion?"

—"Go ahead, ma'am, but I don't know if I can take it. I'm already kind of wobbly in the knees."

—"Let's unload my boat from the trailer and cruise out on the lake together and see what develops. Who knows, we might get lucky and find ourselves some walleyes."

—"That sounds like a pretty good deal to me, ma'am."

 ## WHAT HAPPENS AFTER COURTSHIP

In the later courtship stage, after the initial passionate encounter, repeated body contact can often occur, even in Minnesota. I wish I could be more specific about it, but I don't think it's any of your business. One thing we're not in Minnesota is exhibitionists. You'll just have to wing it and do the best you can.

The wedding ceremony stage of a Minnesota romance is an open book. But if you get married in Minnesota, don't expect grade-A hoopla. We're not big on hoopla. Bridal boutiques are not a growth industry here.

What follows is the text of a complete Minnesota wedding. There are several other models to choose from, but they're basically the same.

—"Do you, Jeff, pretty much promise to honor and obey Julie, and take her to be your lawfully wedded wife, as far as that goes then?"

—"Yeah, good deal."

—"And you, Julie, do you pretty much take Jeff to be your lawfully wedded husband then?"

—"Whatever."

—"That does it, then, kids. You can kiss if you want. And let me say that I hope this marriage is a heckuva deal for both of you."

Simple, yes, but it covers all the bases. If you get more elaborate, you can lose sight of the real meaning, and that can lead to trouble. Put on your duds, get to the church, get it over with, and drive on out of there. That's my advice.

The Minnesota Honeymoon

Very little is known about Minnesota honeymoons or the sex life of Minnesotans in general. I mean we all know about our own, but we don't discuss it with anybody. Ten or eleven years ago a man and woman from Harvard came out here to study sexual patterns in Minnesota. They stayed a year, interviewed over 1,200 Minnesotans, and ended up with a single page of conclusive statistics that got them fired from their department.

Another sort of touchy subject. A guy from Illinois told me one day, "You've got massage parlors in the big cities just like us. What makes you think you're so high and mighty and moral?" I didn't say a word, I just gave him ten dollars and sent him through the doors of the Velvet Curtain Massage Inn. He was back out in ten minutes.

—"You people are sick. Do you know what they did in there? They sat me on a folding chair fully clothed and then removed my glasses and rubbed my temples."

I could've told him that's what they'd do, but he would not have believed it.

 ## WHERE TO GO IN MINNESOTA

The Missing Bedroom

[*Note*: I've seen it with my own eyes, the Missing Bedroom. I don't know if you should make a special trip, but if you're headed toward western Minnesota and you get to the Montevideo area, just look for the signs or ask anybody how to get there. It's an ordinary old farmhouse, but you can clearly tell where Jack Ikeson's bedroom used to be. It's quite the mystery. The story reprinted below is based on interviews with Jack before he died in 1984. The bedroom turned up missing on October 9, 1977. —H.M.]

It was late when bachelor farmer Jack Ikeson pulled into his yard. He had been playing cards at the pool hall—some whist, but mostly buck euchre. He went inside and made himself an onion-and-blue-cheese sandwich and ate it with his workboots off while he read the comics. After seventy-three years, it was still his only vice, he told people. He had no use for whisky and he only smoked at weddings.

After his snack, he undressed in the living room and draped his clothes over the wooden chair next to the telephone-cable spool he used for a table. He took his longjohns off the hook by the radio and put them on for pajamas. He walked to the bedroom door, turned the glass knob, pushed the door open, and brought his right foot forward across the sill.

Jack's farmhouse was built at the turn of the century and was meant to function as shelter, little more. There is a dirt-floor cellar under the living room with a trapdoor near the west window. That's where Jack went during storms that could produce tornadoes. That's where he stored his onions and potatoes, in sacks hanging from nails pounded into the joists. The other rooms of the house have crawl spaces under them. Theoretically a person could crawl under there, but Jack never did. There was no reason to. Mice crawled there, and, from time to time, a larger animal. Jack could have kept the mice out of his crawl space if he had patched up the rock foundation, but patching it was not high on his list of things to do. In fact he never had a list of things to do.

At night, as he lay in bed, Jack could hear the mice running around in the crawl space and cellar. They were having fun, jumping and squeaking. He tried poison, but the mice would then just die under the floors or in the walls and the smell would take a long time to go away. In the fall, when Jack would see the first mouse scoot along the baseboard in the kitchen, he would bait some snap traps with hamburger or candy bars, whatever was handy. He put one behind the refrigerator, another on the top shelf of the cupboard where he kept the sugar, and one in the bread drawer. After he ran his trap line for a few days, the mouse populace would be back in the crawl space.

Jack's friends told him the mice would burn his house down someday chewing on an electrical wire. He said it was a chance he was willing to take.

Jack's bare foot stepped only on air after he brought it

forward through the door. The bedroom was gone. No ceiling, no roof, no floor, no bed. Nothing was left except the rock foundation and the dirt of the crawl space, eighteen inches below the doorsill. The south wall of the bedroom was the north wall of the living room and was intact. The framed picture of his parents had not budged.

In town you could hear it different ways. Some people had him surprised by the cool blast of night air when he opened the bedroom door. But that was no surprise to a man who liked to sleep where he could see his breath.

The truth was, when he opened the door and his right foot came down past where the floor had been for years, Jack's immediate thought was that he had made a mistake of tremendous proportions. Whatever was happening, it was his fault. And then he thought: *Let go of the knob and roll.* He lowered his right shoulder, tucked in his chin, and managed to land on his upper back in the dirt. He turned one complete somersault and part of another before he stopped with his feet propped against the rock foundation of what was once his bedroom. He could see the stars. He could see the big box-elder tree by the chicken shed.

When he told it to his cronies at the pool hall, he said he had sworn out loud, "*Where in hell did my bedroom go?*" But he didn't. He didn't say a word as he lay there. He was breathing so hard his whole body was vibrating. He looked back over his shoulder and saw the door from the living room hanging open. He stood up, dusted himself off, stepped over the foundation wall, and drove to town in his longjohns, where he called the sheriff from the pay phone in front of the post office.

The bedroom was gone. The sheriff took a picture of it not being there. He even had his deputies looking for the bedroom, but it never turned up. Most people wrote it off as an elaborate prank.

Jack often wondered why he hadn't just kept the whole thing to himself. He lived in the house until he died and slept in the living room on a bed made from an old feed bunker. Sometimes at night he would walk over and open the door to the bedroom and stand there looking out at the grove of trees. Sometimes it made him wish he had married.

A Big Thank-You to Raw Bits™

Without RAW BITS as a sustaining sponsor it would have been tough going to pay all the bills associated with writing the original *How to Talk Minnesotan* and having it printed. I am happy to say that RAW BITS has stepped up to the plate once again. Charlie T, the CEO, laid it out for me: "Our sales increased year by year after your visitor's guide made its debut. The bulk of our new customers learned about RAW BITS from the ads in your book and said as much in postscripts to their qualifying stories."

If you are new to RAW BITS, you should know that it is not sold in stores and is never discounted or sold by Amazon or Walmart. To qualify for monthly shipments of RAW BITS, applicants will be accepted by invitation only from the RAW BITS Company after they submit two references and an acceptable account of a life event as determined by the board of directors.

Back in late 1987 Charlie T sent me a one-pound sample of RAW BITS so I would be able to field gustatory questions about the product from readers, since it would be promoted in my book. I like RAW BITS, especially for breakfast, and sometimes for an evening snack. Charlie T made me the first ever honorary customer, but I pay cash like everybody else, no discount or expedited shipping by FedEx. RAW BITS is a no-perks company, and that goes for Charlie as well.

ALERT: A product emerged in 2007 calling itself GNAW BITS, which you are welcome to try, but don't forget to read the label concerning a potential gagging and sneezing hazard connected with the dried peas and ragweed seeds listed in the ingredients. RAW GRITS, another knockoff, showed up in 2010, with production by a Georgia company that also manufactures fiberboard and paneling. As far as we know, RAW GRITS consisted of a sawdust-like substance sweetened by high fructose corn syrup, okra chips, lard, and marshmallows. It is gluten free. Or I should say was. The FDA banned the product in 2011, but it soon reemerged as a quick-start product for fireplaces and wood-burning heaters.

Gambling in the Schools

When the state of Minnesota jumped into legalized gambling, it was off the deep end without a lifeguard, as Harold Mire likes to say. Canterbury Downs (now called Canterbury Park) was first out of the chutes as a clean, well-lit horse track with betting that had a family feel to it, but soon expanded to offtrack betting with simulcasts that made it feel like New Jersey. In 2012 Canterbury Park might as well be called a casino, since it does have a variety of card games including blackjack, Texas hold 'em, and many more. Current legislation allows Canterbury Park to have only fifty card tables and horse racing. For some reason Canterbury cannot have slot machines. I almost forgot the Minnesota Lottery, the biggest gamble of all, operated by the state of Minnesota.

There came a day a few years ago when the legislature was behind on its annual responsibility to fund public schools, with the clock running down to session end. The legislators were instead wrestling with the tough math question of how many video gaming devices bars and restaurants could legally have on their premises.

"Gambling in the Schools" appeared on the Sunday *Star Tribune* commentary page with a byline familiar to the *Strib* readers. Somebody was sticking his/her neck out once again, though I could have warned him/her that the use of irony has its drawbacks, and in a newspaper especially, irony has trouble written all over it. As it happened, several readers thought that the legislature had actually passed the bill. Several people phoned their elected legislators, furious that this had happened without consulting Minnesota citizens first. It was a learning experience for the author, the legislature, and the readers, who should have had their big cup of coffee before they turned to the commentary page that Sunday morning. —H.M.

The Education Gambling Bill

Parents and teachers who have been worried sick about finding enough money just to maintain public schools at a minimal level or better, worry no more.

The Minnesota legislature recently approved the Education Gambling Bill, which allows video gaming devices (VGDs) in K–12 classrooms.

Only two machines per classroom will be permitted, unless the class size exceeds thirty, in which case one additional VGD will be permitted for each additional ten students.

Class size, however, will not be a problem once the gambling revenue begins pouring in.

Students in math classes will be instructed in probability, statistics, and hot streaks.

The VGDs in kindergarten classrooms will operate with nickels only.

All students will be expected to do their assignments and homework before gambling, unless they're on a roll.

Powerball and Gopher 5 lottery tickets will be sold only in the lunchroom during the noon hour. The attractive neon Minnesota Lottery signs will be permitted at the main entrance of the school and near the scoreboard at games.

Pull tabs and scratch-offs are specifically outlawed in the bill because they make a big mess, according to the powerful janitors lobby.

Offtrack horse betting will be handled in the principal's office, with a two-dollar and five-dollar window initially, but with the option of a hundred-dollar window after the first year.

Race results from the major American tracks will be broadcast to the students on the classroom Channel One.

National scratch sheets will be available in convenient locations. The first half hour of the school day will be a "handicapping homeroom," but students will be encouraged to arrive early if they are psyched up and have the feeling this is the day.

Each school system may publish and sell its own tip sheet or it can hire a professional tipster, such as "Gimp" Gordon or "Fast-Forward" Freddy, to be a counselor and role model.

Betting on high school sports will be forbidden, but the morning line for collegiate and professional sports will be broadcast on Channel One and posted in the principal's office near the sports-betting window.

As a safeguard, students will not be allowed to bet on sporting contests unless they have successfully passed Math II: Point Spreads and Injuries.

Poker games will be operated as an extracurricular activity from the final bell until 4:00 A.M. The school will be the "house" and provide the dealers.

There will be a 10 percent rake-off for each pot up to a maximum of ten dollars per hand. Only 5-card draw, stud, and hold 'em will be permitted.

Midnight Baseball, Spit in the Ocean, or Mission Impossible will not be permitted because they are silly games of chance and would send the wrong message to students.

Gambling will obviously bring new life and big money to the schools, but there are other advantages:

1. Students will be prepared for jobs in the gambling industry after graduating.
2. Jobs will be created in the schools for change walkers, dealers, security officers, and so on.
3. A wider variety of people will be attracted to the teaching profession.
4. Discipline will improve because the hope of getting something for nothing is one of the oldest drives for excellence.

Lesson 17

Living Off the Land,
Snowbirds, and So ... Then

TALKING WITH SNOWBIRDS

If you live in Florida or Texas or Arizona, you can practice Minnesotan without leaving your state by finding some snow-birds to talk to. Snowbirds are Minnesotans who abandon us in the winter and head south with the birds. They love to talk about home because they feel so guilty and ashamed for having left it.

A guy we'll call Kyle from a town in Yellow Medicine County retired when he was sixty-three and said he wouldn't live anyplace but Minnesota. His first winter in retirement, he stayed put. The second year, he and his wife sneaked off to Florida for a couple of weeks. "A little vacation—the heat made me feel sick, though." The next year Kyle and his wife spent January in Florida: "January's kind of rough on us. We like to stay around for the holidays, then get a little sun, and then come back to where our roots are." The next year it was January and February. "No sense driving back before March. You never know what you'll run into. In some ways it's cheaper to live there. We're partners in a little trailer home."

The year after that, they decided that they could suffer through Christmas in Florida if they worked at it—they would leave after Thanksgiving. But that year they had the car packed on Saturday and got walloped by the traditional Turkey Blizzard. Blizzards have struck eight out of ten Thanksgiving weekends for over a century in Minnesota. Kyle looked it up. "Let's go just after Halloween next year." And they did.

They finally rounded it off to six months, October through March. "It's easier to keep track of."

But it's not easy on them when they come back in April.

"Kyle, I see you're back," somebody will say. Somebody else delivers the punch line: "Were you gone, Kyle? I didn't even miss you."

Around mid-August, at the café where Kyle drops in for coffee twice a day, the boys start giving him a rough time. "It dropped below 60 last night, Kyle. That's kind of chilly for you, isn't it? You could catch cold."

Neither one of them needs to be given a rough time because they already feel bad enough about spending half the year in Florida. Golfing in the winter makes them feel guilty. Having an air conditioner on in the winter makes them feel guilty. Hardly a day passes when Kyle doesn't say to his wife, "If we'd just have about two or three inches of snow every so often so I could help scoop the walks here in Sunshine Village, I think I'd be happier." But I doubt it.

☞ SO ... THEN

The *So . . . then* construction is used to frame many Minnesota questions. In the situation where a person not from around here would ask:

—"Who are you?"

The Minnesotan would ask:

—"So who are you then?"

So . . . then softens the question and gives it a friendly, personal touch, once you get used to it. But when you hear it for the first time—out-of-state people have told me—it can sound real sarcastic, or even snoopy.

Here are some foreign questions followed by their Minnesota equivalent. Try translating the questions yourself before checking the Minnesota version.

THEM: "Why did you buy *that* car?"

US: "So why would anybody in their right mind buy a car like that then?"

T: "Is the whole-life policy a better investment?"

U: "So you're saying if a guy took that whole-life policy it wouldn't be too bad a deal then?"

T: "Should I send these ties to Goodwill?"

U: "So I should just throw out five perfectly good wide paisley ties that match my suit then?"

T: "Where are the tent stakes?"

U: "So, tell me, is it too much to ask that the tent stakes would be in the same place as the tent and the beer cooler then?"

T: "When are you leaving?"

U: "So when do you think you might start making your move toward leaving then?"

T: "When?"

U: "So when then?"

T: "Why?"

U: "So why then?"

T: "Will you take my personal check?"

U: "So I was wondering could you maybe cash this personal check for me if it's not too much trouble then? I'm not a criminal or anything."

T: "Why are you eating candy?"

U: "So does that one-pounder bag of M&Ms you got there in your hand mean that's about it on the diet then?"

T: "You're not going to the family reunion?"

U: "So if they didn't bother to send you an invitation to the reunion even why should you bother to go then?"

In a variation of the basic construction, *So . . . then* can be attached to the front of your statement or question. You are talking to a young couple about to be married:

—"So then it's marriage for you two, is it?"

In long statements, a safe policy to follow is to insert maintenance *thens* periodically. In the following example someone has just given you directions: you would then use one *so* at the beginning and plant *thens* here and there for clarity.

—"So you say I turn right then at the first stoplight and veer left at the curve by the Beauty Shop then, and it's just on the other side of the alley then, or was it the second stoplight then?"

I don't want to make your head spin, but I've got to point out that 99 percent of the time *then* has nothing to do with time and is not the opposite of *now* by a long shot. The following question should clear up the confusion:

—"So what you're trying to tell me is that this is now and that's then then?"

WHERE TO GO IN MINNESOTA

Living Off the Land

[*Note*: My brother farms out in southwestern Minnesota, and since 1968, he has had five different tenants in an old farmhouse at a building site he owns on what he calls "Mortgage Hill." The renters were all young people who wanted to live off the land. My brother had no objection to somebody trying to live off the land. He'd been trying it himself for years.

Three of the tenants lasted less than a month. They all took off the same way: in the night and leaving nothing behind but a lot of marijuana seeds in the carpet. The fourth tenant, a young man, lasted four months—until his VW van caught fire and rolled into the creek. He stuffed his worldly possessions in his backpack and thumbed down the road.

But in 1970 my brother got a tenant who was determined to stay. We all thought he'd make it, but he didn't. After he moved out—thirteen years later—my brother found the following copy of a letter he had evidently sent, or planned to send, to his old friends back in the Twin Cities. I have left off his name. If he happens to read this guide, though, my brother says stop by sometime and tip a couple in the backyard.

It's a pretty sad deal, in a lot of ways, but he didn't lose his sense of humor, even though he lost about everything else. You might find it instructive, especially if you've been toying with the idea of subsistence living in Minnesota. We've got a bunch of abandoned farmhouses for you to choose from if you decide to make your move. —H.M.]

> Dear Friend or Current Resident:
> Surprise.
> When I moved out to the Minnesota prairie in 1970 to start the Great Experiment on four acres of land, you and I promised to stay in touch with each other. I was supposed to be the point man, you recall, for the second big migration, and you had some notion of following me if my reports from

Eden were favorable. You kept your side of the bargain by writing to me until 1979. Off and on I have felt guilty, but it always passed and so did the years. Now it's 1984.

This is my first report.

The recurring question in your later letters boiled down to this: "Did you fall in a pit or something?" I knew what you meant. If it's any consolation, I did fall in a pit, but only once, and I got out of it. It wasn't the reason I never wrote. I don't know why I never wrote.

The pit I fell in was west of the house but it didn't look like a pit, it looked like part of my lawn. In other words it looked like dandelions, quack grass, chamomile, clover, foxtail, and pigweed. Give me some credit—if it had looked like a pit I wouldn't have fallen in it. Actually, I didn't fall in, I sank in. I was walking around the house checking for a strange creaking sound in the siding, when I disappeared into the lawn up to my waist. Under the lawn was an old cistern that had been used as a large garbage can by previous tenants and then covered with dirt when it was full. I'm just thankful the previous tenants didn't operate a nuclear power plant.

I got a lot of mileage out of the cistern story in the early days, but it has worn fairly thin lately, like so much here.

I want you to know that I did reread all your letters before starting mine. Well, not all. The chickens got into the red shed (that's where the overflow from the house goes) in '76 or '77 and pecked holes in most of 1975's letters, causing large gaps of meaning. On top of that, the chickens had added some unusual punctuation. It wasn't the chickens' fault. I left the door open and they hopped in.

I never did keep the chickens in a pen because I wanted them to be free to scratch for crickets

and worms and other natural foods and free to
build their nests where they wanted. That made
egg gathering a little tougher for me, and since
the chickens tended to congregate on the front
stoop during the day, it made walking barefoot
tougher, too.

Which reminds me of the guy whose chewing
gum fell out of his mouth in the chicken yard and
he had to try five pieces before he found the right
one. That joke is one of the big box-office grossers
in this area, and depending on who tells it, the guy
who loses his gum is a carpenter, a schoolteacher, a
hippie, or a Norwegian. It's always a man, though,
and not a woman, which makes sense to me, but I
don't want to explain why I think so.

Your 1975 letters were pecked into nonsense
no later than 1977 because that was the year the
last hen bought the farm. At first I always kept a
rooster with the hens because it was more natural
to eat *fertilized* eggs, according to a brochure I
picked up at the Silver Surfer Food Co-op in town.
Silver Surfer sold only fertilized *brown* eggs.

The co-op was called Silver Surfer because the
board didn't want anybody to confuse it with a
supermarket that sold processed foods, not that
they had anything to worry about. Also, Ben, the
first coordinator of the co-op, had a large collection
of Uncle Scrooge and Silver Surfer comics. He
wanted to call the food co-op Uncle Scrooge but he
compromised. Ben quit during the "Cheese Blowup."
The board had decided that the co-op workers
should wash their hands before they cut the bulk
cheese into chunks for display. Ben said he didn't
wash his hands when he cut cheese at home and he
didn't see why he had to do it at the Silver Surfer.
Telling people to wash their hands violated everything
the co-op stood for. Next thing you know it'll be a
supermarket, he said.

Ben went deeper into the wilderness after that, but when he came out in 1982, I heard he was driving a truck for Coke and taking night classes in computers. The Silver Surfer became the Friendly Food Co-op in 1980 and at present offers a full line of snack foods, some of them with preservatives. There's also orchestra music coming out of the ceiling, and once a week they have a drawing for "Bonus Bucks."

Fertilized egg doesn't sound nearly as appetizing now as it did when I got the first flock, I will say that. Anyway, the rooster always roosted on the rafters above the car in the garage. Getting up there was not easy for him, because his wings—like the wings on most domestic chickens—were not designed for flying. Modern chickens are bred for meat and eggs, not for wings, the way modern man is bred for watching TV and drinking beer. The modern chicken starts running and flapping its wings until it's airborne, in a manner of speaking, but it's about as aerodynamically sound as a St. Bernard. The rooster was overweight besides. It took ten minutes of clawing and flapping for him to reach the rafters at sunset. It was something you didn't like to watch too many times. Everything is beautiful in its own way except for a fat rooster going to roost or modern man watching *Monday Night Football* from a lounge chair.

The rooster got so it couldn't distinguish between the rising sun and the yardlight. Intelligence is not a chicken's strong suit. Four or five times a night the rooster would thud and flap onto the hood of the old Nash and go out under the yardlight and crow because he thought it was morning. I probably could have adapted to it, but that rooster's crow was not your fairy-tale "cock-a-doodle-doo." It was a cross between a plugged sump pump and a TV evangelist with tight underwear. To make a long story as short and as pleasant as possible, let me just say the rooster eventually ended up in the food freezer, after expiring suddenly one morning about 3:30 under his beloved yardlight. The hens, one by one, fell victim to the fox and the weasel.

After that I began buying unfertilized white eggs in plastic cartons. I didn't know it then, but that was the first step on the long downward trail of moral erosion.

And whatever happened to Cathy, you've asked in your letters. Our first and only winter together, we had a vicious blizzard. On the north side of the house there was a large hole under the eaves that the squirrels used as a door into their play area, but we didn't know that. The attic above the bathroom drifted full of snow. We didn't know that either, until the mid-January thaw.

The plaster ceiling of the bathroom disintegrated and collapsed. I put up some plastic sheeting and positioned peanut butter tubs under the big drips, but still the water would plop on us when we least expected it. It was really the last good laugh Cathy and I had together. The next blizzard in early February knocked out our electrical power for ten days. The first day we snuggled and read Kurt Vonnegut to each other, but on the third day Cathy withdrew into herself. In March, she moved to Long Beach and eventually started a gift boutique with a loan from her father. We wrote back and forth for a few months. You know how it goes.

My original philosophy about living on the land came partly from the *Mother Earth News*, but most of it came from *Catch-22*. My hero was Orr, the WWII bomber pilot who always crash landed on every mission because it was good practice in case he ever had to crash-land. And that's what I figured I was doing here on the prairies: I was living the simple life on the land because it was good practice in case I ever had to live the simple life on the land.

That philosophy has its flaws, I see that now. Take the skunks. At present, I see no reason why I had to practice removing skunks from under my house. But back then I was more idealistic. So when I came home from town one night in May after Cathy left, the house was filled with the smell of skunks (they had been mating under the house). I didn't even think about looking in the Yellow Pages. And how would I have paid Acme Skunk Eradicators anyway? With fertilized eggs?

Getting twelve skunks (the final count) out of the cellar and crawl spaces under the floors was just one more episode in the saga of self-sufficiency. For your information, this is part of what you need for skunk removal: steel traps, hamburger, command post of hay bales, red eyes from staying up all night, shovel. I would rather not go into details.

Maybe some people would say it was inevitable, but there came a point finally when I stopped practicing and decided to make a permanent crash landing. It wasn't the skunks or fertilized eggs that finally did it, and it wasn't the gophers chewing through the pump wires, or the squirrels in the ceiling. It was the garden. I never thought it would be the garden. It was like being cheated by a priest in a poker game or struck by a pacifist. You don't expect it and it's such a shock.

From the beginning the garden was the centerpiece of the experiment, the jewel in the crown. The idea was to grow everything I needed. You can't grow cheese or yogurt, so I bought milk products with the understanding that I could easily do without them. Animal protein was not a big concern for me either, but every so often that first year I would wake up with this craving for barbecued pork ribs and a pitcher of draft beer. But I knew that barbecued pork ribs were not necessary for life, and neither was Grain Belt beer. The beer I brewed in a plastic tub was plenty serviceable if you didn't drink the sludge that formed in the bottom.

By the third year my garden had expanded to half an acre and I had shifted from a spade to a gasoline-powered Rototiller (I felt bad about it). I had two compost heaps and a never-ending supply of sheep manure from a neighbor. Nothing made me happier than a wheelbarrow full of sheep manure. Those were the days.

What more could a person want? Half the year I was studying seed catalogs and the other half I was working in the garden. I grew northern jumbo peanuts, kale, Jerusalem artichokes, lima beans, four varieties of lettuce, three varieties of carrots. You name it, I planted it, cultivated it, watered it, mulched it, harvested it, stored it. Except rice. The rice paddy was a miserable flop and it took its toll.

Last year I grew only potatoes, carrots, onions, tomatoes, and lettuce. But when the seed catalogs started coming in January this year I decided I had practiced gardening long enough. I knew how to do it in case I ever had to do it. I didn't order my seeds. I've got a few jars of canned tomatoes in the cellar, but when they're gone, it's back to the grocery store, not back to the land.

My plans are to return to the Twin Cities in September. Maybe I'll see you around. I apologize again for not writing sooner, but look on the bright side, I saved you a lot of trouble.

This is my last report.

IRONCLAD PAJAMAS

IRONCLAD. The steel-belted sleepwear built to take it... and we mean all that flip-flopping you do when you're sound asleep. If you're wearing ordinary over-the-counter pajamas that blow out in the knees and look like wadded Kleenex after a couple of weeks in the sack, you need a pair of industrial strength IRONCLAD PJs. IRONCLADS never fail under stress, even if you do. Every pair of IRONCLADS is run over by a bulldozer and then filled with 200 pounds of sand and dropped off a twenty-story building—yet the elastic in the waistband still has plenty of snap.

IRONCLAD PJs, the four-ply polyester steel-belted pajamas you buy with confidence ... you'll need a new mattress and bed long before you'll need new pajamas, if you're wearing IRONCLADS when you hit the hay.

Howard Mohr

MINNESOTA FARMING: AN UPDATE

In 1987 when *How to Talk Minnesotan* was published, farming at the basic level in Minnesota had not changed all that much for years. Farmers planted corn, soybeans, and small grains, such as wheat or oats, all of which were food crops for the consumption of human beings and livestock, such as cattle and hogs, and milk cows. The cattle and hogs, for your information, became beef and pork at some point and were then eaten by human beings, a repetitive cycle that inspired many to think that farming was the good life. A farmer could make a decent living in spite of the ever-increasing prices for machinery—another thing, besides the weather and the grain markets, they could not control.

Agra Sci-Fi

Farmers had for decades been buying hybrid seeds for spring planting. But what emerged like wildfire in the waning twentieth century were seeds designed in the laboratory by gene-splicing for particular purposes. By making a corn seed whose plant could tolerate a powerful herbicide, a farmer could watch his corn come up, and as soon as the weeds appeared, he could spray the crop, killing the weeds, but not the corn. A corn seed incorporating genetic material from a pesticide is also used to control rootworm, a crop-damaging bug. The value to the farmer is that he does not have to spend so much time cultivating crops to remove weeds, nor does he have to spray pesticide on the crop, since it is "built in." Gene-spliced seeds are more expensive, thereby becoming one more thing farmers can't control.

Global Positioning Satellites in Modern Farming

Minnesota farmers began using GPS to plant and harvest their crops, collecting valuable data on crop yields. The GPS tractor has a cab-mounted screen and software for placing the tractor on autopilot. GPS tractors automatically move over the fields with very little input from the farmer except to respond to the familiar woman's voice from the computer in case of a computer glitch: "Recalibrate! Recalibrate!" The crop can be planted, cultivated, and harvested accurately by GPS. A farmer in 2012 using GPS will have by now stored the data from all his fields into the hard drive of the computer and backed it up on his laptop or iPad. Needless to say, the cost of a GPS tractor, not to mention the software, puts quite a dent into the budget, and yes, it's another expense farmers can't control.

GPS farming is a national and global phenomenon. But one Minnesota GPS farmer has made a profitable break-through writing popular fiction. George Minster (his pen name) is a southwestern Minnesotan farmer in the Hanley Falls area who was somewhat addicted to reading mysteries while letting his tractor do the driving by GPS, but like most Minnesota farmers, he didn't want his neighbors to think all he did was ride around with his nose in a book, sipping coffee, checking e-mail, noodling on his guitar, and streaming old John Wayne movies. He figured that he could write mysteries as well as the next guy. In his GPS-guided tractor George had plenty of time to crank out "Keeping the Lid on Larceny," "It's in the Blood," and "Facebooking with a Corpse," all best sellers featuring "Ole's the Name," his popular grain farmer turned private investigator. George's newest, "You Bet He's Dead," should be in the stores by late 2013.

Public Service Notice: Genetically Engineered Farmer Rumors

Maybe you've read the scandalous stories, or watched Fox News, suggesting that some farmers in Minnesota have signed up to be genetically modified for the new age of farming, allowing them to pass on their valuable GPS-ready spliced DNA to their children and grandchildren. This is completely false.

And the same goes for the stories about Minnesota farmers sitting in lawn chairs beside the field, shirt off, taking in the rays, using a remote to guide the GPS tractor on its task of prepping the soil and planting the grain. The color photo of Minnesota farmer Ricky Crickson using a remote and sipping a gin and tonic made the rounds on Facebook, but you should know that he has never had a G & T in his life, and that his neighbor photoshopped that inglorious picture.

Please share this notice with others on social media. Just say NO to silly fabrications.

Lesson 18

Wyoming, Golf, and the Law, Minnesota-Style

 ## A SPECIAL NOTE FOR VISITORS FROM STATES LIKE WYOMING

Now I don't think for a minute that Minnesota has the corner on being fairly friendly and low-keyed, but even if you come from a state known for these qualities—say, Wyoming or Texas—you should take your lowest key and then drop it an octave or two when you visit us. We can have just as good a time as anybody in Wyoming, and almost anybody in Texas. So just go ahead and say what comes naturally:

> —"Boy, one night last week a bunch of us piled in the pickup, drove into Cheyenne, partied all night, shut a couple of places down, and got back to the ranch just in time to saddle up."

No problem. A Minnesotan would get right in the spirit of that remark and reply like this:

> —"Yeah, I tell you. The other night I went to the Fire Hall pancake feed and then afterwards a bunch of us sat around and played cards right through the 10 o'clock news. I was really tired the next day."

The use of exaggeration is slightly different in Minnesota. Here's an exchange between a Minnesotan and a visitor from Wyoming.

—"So, how big is this ranch of yours?"

—"We call 'em farms here in Minnesota. I farm 400 acres."

—"Four hundred acres!!?? My *lawn* back home is bigger than that. My kiddos got a hundred acres just for their sandbox!!!"

—"You bet. That's a big sandbox. Must be a full-time job just keeping the cats out."

—"I thought maybe I'd do a little hunting while I'm here. You know back home the elk are so thick, we just open a window and fire. Think I could get myself an elk in Minnesota?"

—"If you're a good hunter. We had three elk living in Minnesota last year, but two of 'em walked over the border into South Dakota and the other one hasn't been seen for a while. That's the one you'd have to get."

Easy, isn't it? Just be glad you're not from California. Californians have a terrible time learning how to speak and act Minnesotan. The funny thing is, a lot of them were Minnesotans who moved out there to strike it rich or stay warm—but something happened. When they came back for a visit, they act like they've been brainwashed. It's not their fault. And that's not to say I don't like California. Don't get me wrong.

By the way, if you want some help on a translation between your state language and Minnesota's, feel free to drop me a line with your question. Please include a SASE.

 # WHERE TO GO IN MINNESOTA

Golfing

After many years of jokes about how so-and-so should just turn his cow pasture into a golf course, and having so-and-so say turning his cows into a golf course would be worth more, so-and-so finally did it, time after time, in small towns across Minnesota. But give us credit—we resisted longer than most civilized cultures.

When push came to shove at the council meetings, though, the big argument was that a golf course would be just the thing to make the town take off again. It would attract businesses. The boards could be taken off a lot of the storefronts. The town would become the focal point for the county. There would be golf tournaments and TV coverage. You never know, it could happen. It hasn't happened yet, but it could.

If a golfing vacation is your idea of a good time, you won't have any adjustments here. Golfing in Minnesota is about what it is in other states. You try to get the ball in the holes in numerical order without cheating and without injuring yourself or those around you. You couldn't invent a simpler game if you tried. Because our courses were built on flat prairie land without trees, a simple game is even simpler. You can see all nine holes from green. That's if you don't count the gopher holes. The pocket gopher is the official state rodent, and as such is a protected species. If your ball goes down a gopher hole, you get a free shot. If you hit a gopher and kill it, there is a one-shot penalty, but you do get your name on the clubhouse wall. If you step in a gopher hole and break your leg, it is an act of God.

 ## BREAKING THE ICE AT MINNESOTA HIGH SCHOOL CLASS REUNIONS

If you've been living someplace else for twenty or thirty years, and you're coming back to Minnesota for a high school reunion, your Minnesotan could be a little rusty. You're bound to have some rough edges. Maybe that's the way you want it, but remember that most of your old classmates did not have the privilege or desire of moving out of state. They're not the strangers—you are. If your purpose in coming back is to offend people and show them how far you've gone, fine, just skip over this part or even the whole book, for that matter; you're probably hopeless. But a lot of people knew that when you left. Don't do anybody any favors.

All the lessons in this guide can be put to good use, but here are some sample openers. After that, you're on your own.

An incorrect ice breaker precedes the correct one. Can you see what's wrong?

—"Brenda, the bald guy on your left with the turkey tie and mayonnaise on his lapel, is that the same husband you've always had? I thought you dumped him."

—"So, Brenda, this is quite the deal then, isn't it? Oh, here's a Kleenex—why don't you give it to the sophisticated-looking gentleman on your left there. Isn't he a TV anchorman?"

—"What crawled up on my plate and died?"

—"Gosh, I haven't had any lutefisk for, I don't know, twenty, twenty-five years. It sure brings back some strong memories."

—"Oh, Dale, I'll never forget that time we accidentally got locked in your uncle's basement and had to spend the whole night there playing Ping-Pong and so forth. Has your wife there heard that one?"

—"Dale, remember me? We rode the same school bus."

—"Richard, do you still think it was me that took the engine out of your car after the prom and pushed it into the lake?"

—"So, Richard, what're you driving these days?"

—"Last I knew, Frank, you were facing embezzlement charges at the bank. How'd you come out on that anyway? I hope it was better than you did when you stole the cheer-leader funds from the principal's office."

—"Been catching any walleyes, Frank?"

 # SOME INFORMATION ABOUT MINNESOTA LAW

If you are called upon to testify in a court of law, or worse, if you are a defendant in a court of law during your stay in Minnesota, I should point out that although our legal system is no more a tangle than anybody else's, you still are judged by factors beyond your control, including how you talk.

When you pick your lawyer, make sure the Minnesota Language Bar Certificate is displayed, or you might as well plead guilty from the beginning and throw yourself on the mercy of the court.

Selected Landmark Rulings in the Minnesota Courts

✓ *The Chicken Suit*

The State Supreme Court, reversing a lower-court decision, has ruled that robbing a bank dressed as a chicken can—in special circumstances—be construed as "goofing off," but the judges hastened to add that they hoped everybody has the sense not to try it again. The ruling came after Ed Olson of Mortwood, Minnesota, rented a chicken suit for the Mortwood Crazy Days. The theme was Farm Funnies. Ed thought it would be a riot if he hopped into the 12th Midwestern Savings & Loan as a 200-pound rooster and demanded a bag of corn from the teller, who at the time was wearing a hog mask and hoof gloves. She pushed the silent alarm, and the guard, in a Henny-Penny costume, hopped over and told Ed to freeze. Ed clucked and flapped his wings and did a couple of turns around the lobby, having a great time until the guard put one bullet into the ceiling fan as a warning.

The Supreme Court ruled that because the bank president was using a bale of hay for a desk and was wearing bib overalls, Ed Olson was thereby within his rights to demand corn from a teller who looked like a hog. They further reprimanded the bank for trying to be funny—it was the court's contention that banks are not meant to be funny places. Ed Olson was chastised and today has a seat in the Minnesota State Legislature, where he can get a laugh any time things slow down by clucking, crowing, and pecking on a tabletop with his nose.

✓ Contracts

A Minnesota District Court ruled that "Well, I don't know—maybe" is legally binding for all practical purposes.

✓ Dark, Brooding Personalities

The same District Court ruled that a person possessing a perpetual gloomy and pessimistic outlook may not be too much fun to be around, but it's not a crime.

✓ Hugs

The Domestic Claims Court of Minnesota ruled in favor of the wife who sued her husband for more hugs. The plaintiff, arguing her own case, proved beyond a shadow of a doubt that her husband never initiated any hugs, and when she hugged him, he drew back and screwed up his face like somebody in pain. The judge sentenced the husband to three years in prison but suspended it on the stipulation that he hug his wife twice a day without being asked, and none of that halfhearted, unaffectionate stuff either. The case is being appealed on the grounds that it violates a Minnesota man's constitutional right to be unemotional.

SELECTED MINNESOTA PRODUCT AND SERVICE DISCLAIMERS

Northstar Typewriter

We assume no responsibility for the words made from the alphabet on the Northstar Typewriter, or for any combinations of those words in sentences, paragraphs, poems, novels, cute essays, or editorials. Nor do we in any way imply that the purchase of this machine will make you a writer or lead the way to a big contract with a publisher. Furthermore, Northstar Typewriter, Inc., and its agents are specifically exempt from blame in the willful or accidental construction of revolutionary statements, obscene words, or ads for banks. We are not liable for the vagaries of authorship or the deep and oppressive gloom that descends on those individuals who sit by themselves before this typewriter day after day. Any harm that comes to the owner of the Northstar Typewriter or to any other person as the direct or indirect result of something printed first by said machine is solely the problem of the person who puts the paper in the roller and pushes the keys. We hope you have many happy typing hours on the Northstar, but of course we cannot guarantee it.

Church Fan

This folding fan was placed in the hymnal rack for your worshipping comfort, compliments of the Pearl Brothers Mortuary. We would be pleased if you would exercise caution in the intended use of this, our flowered fan. Taken in hand, it should be waved to and fro in an arc in such a manner that a gust, you might say, of wind will cross your face. Inordinate velocity could, we are sorry to inform you, cause the fan to fly apart, sending sharp remnants of cardboard into the next pew or farther. It is with deep sorrow that we disavow responsibility for any injury—either psychological, physical, or moral—that results from our tasteful fan impacting with your body or that of another through improper deployment. It also grieves us to make known that although our fan can indeed make you cooler through convection and evaporation, it has its limits. Therefore, we cannot be liable for heat stroke, sleepiness, or sticky underwear. Remember Pearl Brothers Mortuary in your time of need. Your rites may vary in some areas.

Minnesota Birth Certificate

The enclosed birth certificate remains valid for the lifetime of the owner or until death, whichever comes first. You can't blame us if things don't go just like you want after you're born. We're only trying to do our job here, but it gets harder every day because of the cutbacks we suffered. Everybody has to take the knocks and nobody has the right to go around bellyaching about stomach gas, bowlegs, or cowlicks. We certify that you were born of parents—more or less—at a specific time, in a specific place, in a specific county. All the rest is on your shoulders, chum. Welcome to the club.

Have a Nice Day

In saying "Have a nice day" to you, I don't mean to imply that the phrase itself will always affect your day in a positive way. In fact, it could have the opposite effect. Sometimes when I say "Have a nice day," people will glare at me. In one instance I was struck on the forehead with a peanut-butter sandwich. Listen, I sincerely want you to have a nice day when I say so, but if you can't or won't, hey, it's okay, I've been there. Have a nice day.

A Modern Minnesota Marriage Vow

We will love and cherish until death does us part, unless in the meantime we begin to get on each other's nerves. Sickness and sorrow must be shared, along with cleaning the crusty stuff off the bottom of the oven. If communication breaks down or we are nauseous in each other's presence, the holy bond of wedlock may be broken. We expect a couple of super years and three or four pretty good years until our next marriage, but if it seems like it's not quite the deal we imagined, we can go our separate ways at the drop of a hat. We agree to adore each other forever, unless one of us changes lifestyles—in that case we'll get together for drinks sometime and then play miniature golf.

TV Weathercasters

In a minute the weather, but first this. In calling ourselves forecasters, the seven trained meteorologists of the WWTO Weather Central Center are only trying to look on the bright side. Sometimes we hit it right on the nose, but that doesn't make up for the times we have egg on our faces. It baffles us as much as it does you, and we all have our doctorates, except Mert, who doesn't know what he's got, but he's taking medication for it. We marshal every state-of-the-art piece of expensive gadgetry in the Weather Central Center to provide you with an accurate picture of the immediate future weatherwise. But weather is an act of God and sometimes we just have to throw up our hands and take our lumps. Sure it's frustrating and humiliating to be wrong about the forecast day after day. But what's worse is when it stays sunny and mild for a week and we're down in the Weather Central basement playing pinochle. But listen to us: it's worth it, every bit of it, when we straighten our tie and take our place in the weather chair near the map and begin to banter with the anchor-person. You may think of us as primarily weather forecasters, but we think of ourselves as primarily comedians. Sure we miss the predictions about 70 percent of the time—nobody's perfect—and maybe a guy with a wet finger and old shrapnel wound could do better, as many of you have written in to say. That doesn't bother us. But when we walk out in front of the cameras with our pointer and you don't laugh, that's what really hurts.

Minnesota College Diploma

The issuance of this college degree to you, by us, the institution whose name is in gold letters at the top under the loon, is a matter of faith. While you were here we could not be held accountable for your ignorance, and now as you leave our halls of ivy and soybeans, we cannot be held accountable for your knowledge. You may be wiser, sadder but wiser, or just sadder, but whatever your condition we must emphasize that when you paid your tuition and bought your first yellow highlighter pen, you entered into a *nolo contendere* agreement with us. We told you that we could not teach you, that you had to teach yourself, that's what education was. If you botched it, too bad. We did what we could in providing a viable environment of cafeteria food, movies, concerts, casino nights, and a chance to interact with the sex of your choice. If you are the same dumbo you were when your parents dropped you off with your suitcases and posters, you've got nobody to blame but yourself. We're running a university here, in case you hadn't noticed.

DIVEBOMBER
HERBICIDE
(A MEGABRUTE COMPANY)

MEGABRUTE—proudly taking lawn chemicals into the twenty-first century.

Weeds a problem in your lawn? Neighbors forming a committee?

THE ANSWER IS DIVEBOMBER

Just spread an inch of the powerful DIVEBOMBER granules on your lawn and you'll be troubled no more by unsightly Teaweed, Florida Beggarnose, Sesbania, Pigweed, Cockleburr, Smartweed, Dumbweed, Bristly Starbur, Panicum, Quackgrass, Ticklegrass, Foxtail, Crabgrass, LobsterLeaf, Bullhead Bean, Croaking Crawdaddy, Sickle Pod, Velvet Dog, Wild Turnip, Purple Dogleg, Ragweed, Iowa Whackowitch, FloozyWart, Creeping Porkbelly, and Nightspreading Chucklehead.

DIVEBOMBER costs more than the lightweights, but isn't a beautiful lawn worth it?

Now DIVEBOMBER is lightly scented with lemon.

[When applying DIVEBOMBER, wear protective clothing, a class-nine respirator, gloves, and goggles. And please follow label directions or you'll be troubled no more by zinnias, roses, elms, squash, peonies, lilacs, snap beans, birds, raspberries, strawberries, carrots, earthworms, radishes, onions, bluegrass, or small pets.]

Lesson 19

Non Sequiturs, Rebuttals, and Gifts

 ## THE MINNESOTA NON SEQUITUR

As you already know, a Minnesota conversation can sometimes be a series of statements on a common theme: one person's statement leads to a response from another person, as in this discussion of Dutch Elm disease by two native Minnesotans.

—"That big elm of mine over the front porch there doesn't look too perky."

—"I got one like that. They say a guy can pour a couple jugs of bleach around the roots. I don't know."

—"I tried the bleach. Then I called the County Ag Extension office and they had me smear the trunk with Cool Whip—they said some people've been having pretty good luck with the whipped topping."

—"A guy gets desperate all right."

Most Minnesota conversations do not, however, need a common theme. The only rule is to pause briefly between what seem to be disconnected statements.

—"Boy, it's that kind of day. If it were colder you'd be talkin' snow."

[*Pause*]

—"I brought a couple of those retreads for my old Chrysler—I hope they don't peel the way they will."

[*Pause*]

—"Muskmelon. I like it, but it doesn't like me. Upsets my stomach to beat the band."

[*Pause*]

—"I used to keep my billfold in the back pocket of my pants, but then I saw this documentary on pickpockets and now I keep it in the front pocket."

This peculiarity of the Minnesotan language was picked up some years ago by Samuel Beckett (he spent a week near Worthington, Minnesota, when his car broke down). He wrote the first draft of his most famous play in a motel room that looked out on a bare field. He called it *Waiting for the Mechanic*.

I saw a touring production of *Waiting for the Mechanic* at a community theater once. I won the ticket in a radio contest when I guessed how many bottles of Pepsi were in a '55 Chevy driven by a girl in a bathing suit. There are these characters on a stage with no scenery except a couple of pine boards nailed together and a sun hanging from a wire. What happens is, one guy says something in a monotone—"I don't know, it could be the alternator"—and the other guy waits until the drum is struck and then he says in a monotone, "The fruit is balanced on the vestibule." It went on like that for almost three hours. I was fascinated.

Evidently people had walked out on *Waiting for the Mechanic* in some places, but the Minnesota crowd I was with stayed right down to the last beat of the drum. I've seen a lot worse plays in community theaters. I guess I still don't recommend the play.

CONTROVERSY IN MINNESOTA

Phrase

✓ *Yeahbut*

One natural response to a controversial statement in Minnesota is to end the discussion by saying *that's different*. Delivering an apparent non sequitur has the same effect. But there does come a time when you're forced to speak your mind and that's where *yeahbut* comes in handy.

Pronounced "ee-ah-but," *yeahbut* is the introductory phrase in the majority of Minnesota rebuttals. A Minnesota debate consists of a controversial statement by one person and a *yeahbuttal* by another.

—"It's a big country, China, all those people. A guy kinda wonders."

—"Yeahbut they're drinking Coke and Pepsi now, so that's something."

—"I'm using Gasahol in my pickup and I get a good five miles per gallon more out of it."

—"Yeahbut they said it can clog your lines and burn out your valves."

—"You need some recreation. You should try playing golf."

—"Yeahbut there's always the danger I might start liking it."

After the statement and the *yeahbuttal*, just leave it alone. Drop it. Don't keep harping.

GIVING AND ACCEPTING GIFTS

Christmas is a time of stress in Minnesota, organized as it is around the giving of gifts. The giving part isn't so bad—we like giving gifts. But it's a two-way street, and eventually somebody will give us a gift in turn or for no reason at all, which is worse. This can lead to hard feelings.

When it comes right down to it, Christmas is a tough one all the way around for most Minnesotans, because although we believe in being of good cheer, we don't think, as a rule, it's a healthy idea in excess. I think what happens is that our natural tendency to keep a neutral point of view and a face to go with it is severely tested at Christmas, and so we draw back and overcompensate. But I'm no psychiatrist.

It comes out in odd ways. Grain elevators like to have a large Christmas star on the highest point, but they leave it up there the year around so it doesn't stand out so much at Christmas. It makes sense to me.

The main idea at Christmas is to get the gift stuff out of the way as efficiently as possible with the least amount of trouble. On Christmas morning the gifts are distributed and opened, and then lined up for everybody to see. The paper and boxes are burned, and it's time for breakfast. It's not unusual to see Minnesotans working at little jobs on Christmas, like changing the oil in the car, cleaning the garage.

The key in all this is to pretend that the holiday is like any other day. Treat it special and pretty soon you're sitting around eating fudge and watching parades on television, and by the end of the day you feel like something the cat dragged in and left on the floor. It can ruin the next day, too.

The best advice: get it done and go on to normal things.

Giving the Gift

When you give a gift to a Minnesotan, be calm, keep your voice down, and avoid eye contact. Don't say the word *gift* during the transaction. Also never wrap the gift, it only aggravates the situation. If you feel you have to wrap it, use old

newspapers or butcher paper, and don't mess around getting
the ends neat. Leave off the bows.

—"Here, take it."

—"What is this?"

—"Oh, something."

—"What's the deal anyway?"

—"I don't know, maybe you won't like it. It's no big
deal."

—"Well, I hope not."

When Minnesotans say "You shouldn't have," they mean
it, because essentially all you've done is make them feel guilty.
It can also backfire on you at any time.

—"Here you go."

—"What're you doing?"

—"Oh, it's just something I brought you from home. It's
nothing. I didn't wrap it."

—"Nothing? It looks like a big box of hand-dipped candy
to me."

—"Yeah, but maybe they're spoiled."

—"I can't take this. You eat the candy."

—"But it's your gift. I just gave it to you."

—"Think I don't know that? So that means it's mine.
Right? So I'm giving it back to you. Here."

—"Well, I appreciate that, I guess."

—"You bet."

This gift-giving transaction was moving along real well
until the gift giver said the word *gift*, you see. That's where it
soured. Let's pick up the dialogue at the trouble spot.

A MINNESOTA DAD'S
XMAS TREE LECTURE

No silver trees. They give me a headache. It's got to be a natural green tree or nothing. I don't want lights on it, they give me a headache, but who ever listens to me. They better not be blinkers, though. We never used to have blinking lights when I was a kid and we were perfectly happy. We didn't even have lights. We strung popcorn on thread for decoration.

If you want the tree, you got to clean up after it. Pine needles are danger-ous. They can stick in your feet and cause infection. You could lose a foot. And another thing, keep that tree watered. When I was your age we did things without being told. Christmas trees can explode into flames without warning. I want you to read the instructions on the fire extinguisher again. If that tree gets dry, out it goes, even if it's Christmas Eve.

And while I'm at it, I don't care what other families do, we're not other fam-ilies. It's dangerous to stack gifts under the tree. They go in the garage until Christmas morning. And don't talk to me about opening the gifts on Christ-mas Eve. We didn't open gifts on Christmas Eve when I was a kid and we were as happy as we had any right to be. And don't go picking at the gifts or shaking and tearing at the corners, or I'll give them all to the neighbors. And that's no idle threat.

And another thing. If you talk to me about outdoor lights hanging off the bushes or the roof of the house, you'll get a big surprise. All it does is en-courage vandalism, and the extension cord is dangerous—the cats could chew on it and electrocute themselves and the ground is frozen, how would we bury them? We could trip on it or hit it with the snow shovel and electro-cute ourselves, and besides it's a waste of electricity, and we never had outdoor lights before and this is no time to start. And if you think I'm kid-ding, you got another think coming. And that's no idle threat.

—"I can't take this. You eat the candy."

—"I'm gonna leave it with you. I'm gonna put it down by your overshoes."

—"You do what you want. But don't expect me to eat it."

—"Eat what?"

—"The candy, there, in the box."

—"Oh, that."

There's no guarantee that the candy will ever be eaten. It may be sitting there by the overshoes next time you visit. If you want to ensure that your gift will be used, make it something that requires no effort on the part of the gift receiver. Extension cords are good. Or light bulbs. Or a couple gallons of milk. Anything that tends to blend in and won't be noticed as a gift.

Accepting a Gift from a Minnesotan

Play it by ear. It's hard to give a gift back to a Minnesotan. Take it, say "You shouldn't have," and put it down someplace. Don't exclaim about it. Eventually it will seem as if it didn't happen.

[*Note*: In regard to Christmas. The "Yes, Virginia, There Is a Santa Claus" letter is rarely reprinted in Minnesota. It's "A Minnesota Dad's Xmas Tree Lecture" that bring tears to many of our eyes during the blessed holiday season. It proves something about us, but what I'm not sure. I'm no psychiatrist, as I said. —H.M.]

Where to Go in Minnesota

 **SANE DAYS**

Some Minnesota communities, in reaction to the proliferation of Midnight Madnesses and Crazy Days that were driving them nuts and to the poorhouse at the same time, came up with Sane Days as an alternative. During Sane Days they don't advertise, put up banners, or dress in costumes.

When you go through a Minnesota town during your visit, if a Sane Day is in progress the signs will be unmistakable. Very few people will be on the streets. The stores will be dimly lit. When you enter, the merchant will say:

—"Are you gonna buy anything?"

If you say "Yes," the merchant will turn on the rest of the lights. Nothing will be on sale. If you buy something, the merchant will ask you if you want a sack for it. No major credit cards will be accepted. That's the way it'll go, shop after shop. Normal, everyday, minimal merchandising. It'll make a nice change of pace for you.

BOB'S B-17 PARK

Bob's B-17 Park—north of Deadwood Falls, Minnesota—has twice received the Medal of the Unusual from the Minnesota Tourist Council. Not that the Council necessarily approves of what Bob is doing out there or that it's the kind of image Minnesota needs, it's just that Bob stands head and shoulders above his competition in the class. But Bob doesn't care one way or another what the Council thinks. He threw the medals in the old matchbox with the paper clips and rubber bands. For that matter, he doesn't care what anybody thinks. He thinks what he wants to, they can think what they want to.

If you come into Deadwood Falls on Highway 29 from either direction, ask anybody how you get to Bob's B-17 Park. If you stop the right person, you'll be personally escorted to Bob's entrance gate and get yourself a pleasant earful besides. If you stop somebody from the other group, they'll say, "Never heard of it." But they have. Everybody has. It's just that there are some killjoys who've been trying for thirty years to change the zoning laws and have Bob's Park—and Bob with it—cleaned up.

There's never a dull moment at Bob's if you are fascinated by old cars and machinery. If Bob does not seem to be home, watch out for the dog. It's called "Dog"—that's what Bob has called all his dogs. He says it's easier to remember and dogs are not particular about names. If Dog comes running out from under the boxcar where Bob lives and hits the chain-link fence at full speed, you would be better off waiting till Bob gets home. Dog's bark is not worse than its bite. Dog never barks. If Bob is home, Dog stays under the boxcar. If Bob is not home, Dog bites whatever comes through the gate. That's what the sign says and you'd better believe it.

When I went out there in the fall of '86—I get out there a couple times a year—I spent the whole day looking at Bob's earth-moving-equipment collection. He could build a freeway on his own if the mood struck him.

He built his own lake in the late '50s with the big Caterpillar bulldozer that he still uses for major maintenance and radical snow removal. He actually built two lakes in the same spot, the second one after the dam washed out on the first one. Bob learned from experience—and so did his neighbors downstream. It's a nice-looking dam and the lake has some fairly good-sized walleyes in it.

One time I was fortunate enough to catch Bob when he was taking out a few tree stumps. That's another thing about Bob. Whatever he's doing, he doesn't stop doing it when you visit. You take potluck. If he's standing in the yard when you show up, then the agenda is open. There are two schools of stump removal, according to Bob. One is to put a logging chain around the stump, hook it to a Caterpillar, and jerk it out. But the other school is dynamite. This is Bob's method of choice. The day I was there, Bob wired eleven stumps with two sticks each while I watched from the cab of the dragline in his yard with binoculars. He pushed the plunger and eleven stumps were separated from the earth, roots and all. I had never seen anything like it. What a show. You should be so lucky on your visit.

If you stop by Bob's on a day when he won't say a word to you, just ask him about his B-17. He bought his B-17 down in Arizona with money he saved up from selling used auto parts and soybeans. He hauled it back to his farm in three large pieces in three long trips in 1963 on an old semitrailer—the trailer is permanently parked in the yard next to the pile driver.

You see the tail section from the road before you see anything else when you drive up the county road that connects to the private dirt road that leads to Bob's. Big American flag on it. Takes your breath away to see that thing out there in the pasture, like it only landed to refuel. If Bob's in a good mood—it's hard to tell one mood from the other with him—he'll let you sit in the top gun turret and push the pedals and rotate the bubble and take aim. He'll even talk to you from the cockpit. "Bogey at two o'clock," he'll tell you over the intercom. You get to wear a leather helmet with goggles, gunner's gloves, the flight suit. Bob's got it all, except live ammunition. But he knows where to get it if he ever needs it. A guy never knows, he says.

The Army made Bob an aircraft mechanic in 1942 when he was eighteen years old and then sent him overseas. When he came back in 1946, he'd seen England, he'd seen France, he'd seen some ladies' underpants, and that was that he said. He was perfectly happy to farm the old family place and tend his garden of cars and machinery. And, since 1963, keep his B-17 operational.

There were people who said Bob was crazy long before he bought the B-17, but after he reassembled the bomber on the hill they called the FBI. The agent they sent out from Washington, D.C., spent two days riding around with Bob on heavy equipment, watched him blow up stumps, and even helped Bob fly a complete mission in the B-17—they took off from England and flew across the Channel without ever leaving the pasture. The agent filed a report at headquarters that gave Bob a top Bureau rating.

Over the years different people have got wild hairs, particularly during the stump season, and made the mistake of calling the FBI again. They've all been told the same thing: *Get off Bob's back, we like him.*

And so do I. He's good company and he never puts on airs. He's exactly what he is. And the only thing that worries me is that one of these days he may put a runway in front of that B-17 with the Cat, fire up all four engines, and take off for parts unknown without so much as a good-bye. But that's Bob for you. He's not real big on ceremony.

Minnesota Minute Mysteries

 MINNESOTA MINUTE MYSTERIES

It is a snowy night in December and you are going door to door trying to make extra cash selling battery-powered aerosol cans. At the last house of the evening, the bell is answered by a little girl about eight years old. She has chocolate all over her face and hands and she says her parents are in the other room. The TV is way too loud, the refrigerator door is open, two dogs are chasing each other through the house. You find the parents in the study, on the floor, with tinkertoys stuck in their ears. *Who did it?*

You are on the road to Grandma's house in a blinding rainstorm. The car is missing—first on one cylinder, then on two. You think you can make it, even after the headlights flicker and the oil light comes on. You can't shift out of second and the radio doesn't work. After passing over a swollen creek, you are now on a section of road with no shoulders. You think you hear a tire making a funny noise. *Is the tire going flat? Is there a jack in the trunk? Or is it back home in the garage with the lug wrench?*

A policeman stops a gray car that didn't come to a full stop at a stop sign. He cautiously approaches the driver's window and asks the driver for his driver's license. The driver reaches over to the glove compartment. The policeman says "Hold it" and draws his gun. The driver sits up real fast, accidentally knocking the car into gear with his shoulder. The car bumps the policeman, causing him to discharge his gun. The bullet travels a

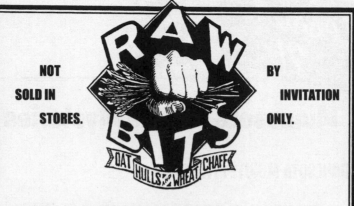
few feet, richochets off the curb, and ends up in the middle of the TV screen of a family watching a rerun of "Love Boat," and it's one they haven't seen. The wall behind the TV set catches fire, so the family evacuates the apartment and calls first the fire department and then the police. Meanwhile the

policeman, who had only heen trying to do his job when he was knocked down, has been nearly run over twice by vehicles whose drivers had scanners. They help the policeman up and call the ambulance. Then they go put a paper bag over the head of the driver who didn't stop at the stop sign. The excitement has made him hyperventilate. The fire truck rounds the corner and hits the police car from behind, pushing it into the produce section of the supermarket across the street. The firemen begin shooting water into the apartment building next to the one where the family was enjoying "Love Boat" so much. The ambulance arrives, skids on the water from the fire hoses, and ends up on the steps of the Episcopal church, where a wedding has just started. The WRT Live-Action News Team comes in overhead in the WRT Action-Copter, televising live to its audience, who have, until then, been watching "Love Boat." The pilot miscalculates and sets down on top of a camper van with tin cans and streamers trailing from its bumper. Everyone at the scene is interviewed. Nobody finds out whether the guy on board with the accent is really a count, as he says, or a realtor trying to impress the secretary who is pretending to be a film star. *Whose rights have been violated here?*

You are happy for once. You are in your car headed for the airport. In the top pocket of your short-sleeved shirt is a round-trip ticket to the Bahamas. You have two weeks. As you turn left at Ninth, a man runs out in front of you, waving his arms. He is wearing only Minnesota Vikings boxer shorts. He appears to be about thirty years old, he is painted purple from the waist up, and red from the waist down. His nose is green. He needs some help, he says. You park the car and go into the house he says is his and you find three people there. One is the wife of the painted man, one is the wife's brother, and the third is the brother's step-uncle. Each is carrying a paintbrush and a can of paint. They are laughing a lot. They say they are interior decorators. *What color is the paint on their brushes? Where did you lose the ticket?*

You are a normal, law-abiding consumer looking for a way to fit good food into your shrinking budget. When the government began requiring expiration dates on foods, you were pleased. Now you could buy something with the confidence that it would last until you got it home. Grocery store owners clearly like the old days better, when the customer took undated food home, though it had an odd taste, but ate it anyway, not knowing it had become the leading character in a science-fiction movie. You have been buying dated food for a few years, wondering if you hadn't died and gone to grocery heaven, when you notice a new problem—besides the fact that some items have as many as four price stickers, one on top of the other. The problem is two-fold, as it often is in sermons. In the first place, food seems to be getting fresher and fresher. That is, the date on the package is further and further into the future, which is where you would

like to be eventually. However, two or three weeks before the expiration date, the package swells up and emits strange gases, like your uncle in Oregon. In the second place, you might buy, say, a tub of cottage cheese on January 9 that has an expiration date of June 12. You take it home, lose sight of it in the refrigerator behind the economy-size jar of pickled-herring chunks and rediscover it on June 7. You open the carton and find the cottage cheese edible, in a manner of speaking. *Have the expiration dates on groceries been made longer so that people will buy the food when it is past being edible and eat it anyway, like in the old days? Or are they putting something in it to make it last longer? Will this make you last longer?*

Lesson 22

Though, Groves, Seniors, and Poker Parties

 **THOUGH**

In the grammar business, of course, we've all been told that it's bad to have dangling participles, and I believe it, though I have never understood exactly what they are. But I do know that in the Minnesota language we have a lot of things that dangle. To me, danglers are words and phrases that are glued on to sentences—they may seem to have no more purpose or meaning than a floating cylindrical article in a bucket of milk, but they are part of what distinguishes a native speaker from an outsider. *Though* is in that category.

— "Did you see her new husband?"

— "He's a good guy, though."

In that exchange, for my money, *though* dangles. The information that would explain the meaning of *though* is missing—and I hate to tell you this, but there's a good chance you won't ever get that missing information, not in this go-around. Those two sentences could be the extent of the conversation about the new husband. The subject would be changed. He's history.

Though is also used in Minnesota to reverse the flow of a longer statement.

— "Those paintings by that guy in town. Ducks, lakes, cabins, sunsets, trees. He's not too bad at it. They say he sells everything he paints. They call him the Picasso of the county, you know. He's better than some of those guys that slap the paint on in streaks and then give it a title like 'Confusion I.' This guy's interested in real stuff. I've never seen any of his paintings, though."

Here's another example—it's the conversational equivalent of being nailed from your blind side when you hear it.

—"Yes, Professor Tidly, I'm doing my essay on capital punishment, the pros and cons of it, and I'm moving along. I looked up the word punishment in *Webster*'s and started there. The encyclopedia would be a good source, too. Plus I'm gonna interview the sheriff and ask my dad and mom about it. I haven't actually starting writing things down on paper, though."

Here's another example:

—"Barney, what a wonderful date. Cheeseburgers. Movie. Riding around in the car. Taking off fast at stoplights. Talking about your plans for the future. I don't want to see you again, though."

Practice with the following one-liners. *Though* should not be pronounced clearly—make it almost "dough," and clip it off.

—"It's hard to row with one oar missing, though."

—"The firetruck got there in time, though."

—"How you gonna keep 'em down on the farm once they've seen St. Paul, though?"

—"Somebody told me they saw him out in the yard in his underwear with a rifle, though."

—"A guy don't want to move too much in this humidity, though."

—"That sermon had some good points, though."

—"It sounded familiar, though."

—"I just don't know, though."

Further Practice

Try alternately tacking *though* and *you bet* on to the end of as many of your Minnesota sentences as possible. Keep doing it until it sounds natural to you. Then try using both at once.

—"I've lived around here all my life, though, you bet."

 # WHERE TO GO IN MINNESOTA

Groves

If you're driving around looking for something to do in Minnesota, you can always stop at somebody's farm and ask to walk through their grove. Hardly anyone charges for the privilege, but watch out for the dogs. Most of the farm dogs in Minnesota are not trained to attack—so don't worry about that. In fact Minnesota farm dogs are not trained to do anything— they're all born with the ability to chase cars and pee on wheels and bark like it was their last chance to bark, which in some cases it is, especially if they try to pee on a moving wheel for variety.

A grove is the stand of trees planted north and northwest of the farmhouse and farm buildings. Its purpose is to protect the owners from the north wind in the winter, and to capture the snow. But since the groves are just a few yards from the house and handy, most people use them as a trash dump. The garbage man does not make the rounds in the prairies. You want to get rid of something—tin cans, baby buggies, old farm machinery, dead cars, lumber—just toss it, drive it, or push it into the grove. If the piles get too high, some people hire a bulldozer to dig a hole every once in a while and push everything in. Then they start over. The groves are built on layers of trash thrown there over the years. And that's where your fun begins.

Wear heavy boots if you get permission to dig in the grove, because broken glass and sharp metal are the standard. What you're looking for out there is the great treasure. Old bottles. Alarm clocks. Anything you can use that the people who threw it in there didn't have any use for. We are born, we throw things away, and then we pass on. It's a funny deal, but that's the way it is.

A shovel is handy, but you can borrow it from the owners. When you drive into the yard, just say where you're from and then ask:

—"Can I dig in your grove?"

If you find something you want, check it out with the owners before you haul it off.

—"You got any use for the handle off this old corn sheller?"

—"Nope—what's it worth to you?"

—"How's a quarter sound?"

—"Good idea—and you can have the bottle for nothing."

—"Thanks—it looks like an antique. What do you think was in it?"

—"Ketchup."

Grove digging. The white man hasn't been in Minnesota long, but he's thrown more trash into the groves and buried it than the Egyptians. So why visit the pyramids when you can walk around in the discarded history of the Minnesota prairies. It can be real instructive if you're in the right mood.

Senior Interviews

[*Note*: The following article first appeared in May 1986, but has been reprinted several times around the state. I include it here because in a few words it says more about our educational system and the kinds of students we are producing than any single document I know of. Senior interviews appear each spring in local papers and are itemized lists of each high school senior's favorite food, most prized possession, and what they would do with a million dollars, among other things. If you plan to move to Minnesota and are worried about what the future holds for your children, this should ease your mind. —H.M.]

School Board President Lauds Seniors

It's heartwarming for me at this time of year to read senior interviews in our little newspaper. The kids put into print their hopes and dreams and fears and wishes. It should make all parents proud and happy.

The favorite subjects this year are Current Events, Shop, and English (with Mr. Borgan). Mr. Borgan comes out as the favorite teacher, but Coach Johnson is not far behind. I expected him to be on top, but this has been a rebuilding year for the fighting Bulldogs and I guess the poor season was reflected in the kids' votes. They say it's not whether you win or lose, it's how you play the game, and I certainly don't blame Coach Johnson, but getting trounced is no fun for the fans. That game with Gilmore made us the laughing-stock of the district. But even then, I think Coach should've talked the team into playing the second half. With a little encouragement I believe they could have made a touchdown. But as it was they all piled in their cars and went home and the superintendent had to announce that the game was over after the pep band played. Something should be done about the officiating, too. I think they were in Gilmore's pocket.

It is odd to see an English teacher so popular, especially a man. But times have changed and that's what makes life interesting. They say he's nice in a strange sort of way. I never did like English. I'm behind Mr. Borgan 100 percent, though.

The favorite movie this year for every senior but one is *Police Academy III*, a very funny movie, and if you haven't seen it, see it. I've seen it three times and laughed harder every time. Darlene, though, liked *Hannah and Her Sisters*, which is not hard to understand if you know her parents, but that's not meant to be a criticism.

The favorite TV show is mostly "Love Boat" or "Falcon Crest" for the girls and "A-Team" or "Miami Vice" for the boys. These are good selections and they are programs with a strong point to make.

Which reminds me. It's good to see that the senior pictures are not those casual snapshots so popular for a while there. In my opinion it took away from the seriousness of the occasion to see a guy with an open-necked shirt just standing there. Or a gal without makeup. Great pictures this year, the boys in sport jackets and the girls all leaning against trees.

For prized possessions, the Trans Am is real popular this year with boys and girls. And nobody picked a foreign car. That's really great. But even more heartening to me is that kids seem to care again and it shows up in their pet peeves. They all said they try to be nice and not judge people, and their pet peeves are people who think they know everything and let you hear about it every day. Or people who aren't concerned with other people or are stuck-up. It's good to see this insight. Back in my day there were kids who thought they were better than anybody else, but we didn't have senior interviews so we could speak out.

Proudest moments this year are the down payment on a Trans Am and All-State Honorable Mention. The favorite sport is basketball. But some kids—even the boys!!—picked volleyball, which we always thought was a sissy sport when I was in school.

The most embarrassing moment for girls seems to be when they showed up on dress-up day wearing jeans. The boys are generally embarrassed by their transmissions going out when they miss a speed shift. Boy, can I identify with that!

I was really surprised when the seniors said what they would do with a million dollars. They all show excellent money-handling ability and a desire to help others. They will pay off the Trans Am first and then upgrade their stereo system, but they would also send their parents on a trip to Hawaii. And they would buy things that were good investments, or put it in the bank at a good rate of return.

Favorite foods are pizza, french fries, french-fried shrimp, chocolate chip cookies, Pepsi, and cheeseburgers.

The advice to underclassmen is excellent this year. You can't worry about everything, so don't worry so much, and remember to have fun your senior year because you are only a senior once, and do the best you can and enjoy life or you may have regrets, especially if you don't try to be yourself.

After graduation, most seniors plan to wait and see what they want to do.

 # WHERE TO GO IN MINNESOTA

Poker Parties

Poker is a popular form of gambling in Minnesota, but the style is a bit different than it is in upstate New York or downstate Florida, probably. I'm only guessing, because I've never put on my lucky feed cap and scooted up to a table in either place. Minnesotans are real fond of poker games that rely heavily on luck. If we played games that relied mainly on skill, we might then have to bear the burden of winning. Winning by luck is hard enough on a guy, but winning by skill is just tempting fate, and we know it.

If you find yourself in a game during your stay here, the following information should help you fit right in without asking too many questions, although if you do ask questions, it won't be that strange, because that's part of the game of poker in Minnesota, along with a lot of shouting and a little lunch every couple of hours.

Here's a simple Minnesota poker test for you. If you pass, you are well on your way to becoming one of us. You are playing five-card draw and are dealt a 2, 8, 9, 10, Q, in four suits. There are three heavy raises and you call them all. At the draw should you toss that 2 and go for the inside straight?

The answer is yes in Minnesota draw. Unless you feel lucky—in which case you should draw three cards and go for the flush. Before either draw you would say:

—"I came to play poker, not watch somebody else play it."

This is your most useful sentence when you're out with the

boys here, even if you're a girl. Folding your hand early is considered bad manners at Minnesota poker parties—you should stay in every hand until the last dog is hung, even if you have to go to the bathroom.

Above all: There's no such thing as a bad hand in Minnesota poker. You look at your hand, you say, "This is a pile of animal waste," and then you bet and say, "I came to play poker."

A Minnesota poker game is called a *poker party.* Calling it a party takes the sinister edge off of it and sets the tone for the good times to follow. A poker party is the men's version of what the women do at the Lutheran church in their circles when they meet on Thursday nights, except that—God love them—the women tend to fold their hands as soon as they arrive and the men don't quote as much scripture.

At every Minnesota poker party there will always be one guy we'll call Orv. He'll be easy to spot. He'll tell you he had to get permission from the War Department to play. The War Department is his wife. She lets him go play because she's glad to get him out from under her feet, as you may understand after you meet him. But she tells him not to come home drunk or take the checkbook with him. Poker parties are right up Orv's alley. He can never remember whether a full house beats four of a kind or if it's the other way around. He has the order of hands on a chart he hauls out of his billfold whenever he has either a full house or four of a kind. It's a tip-off to most of the other players—not that it matters, since he'd bet the same way if he had nothing.

You do have to watch Orv, though. His big weakness is Corn Curls. Once he gets the bag he heads for the bottom.

—"Don't get your head stuck in there, Orv."

The yellow fingerprints on the cards belong mainly to Orv, but by midnight not even an expert witness could tell, because the deck has close to 800 calories stuck to it, including chunks of barbecues and pickle seeds. If you don't have to throw the deck away at the end of the evening or run it through the dishwasher you can figure it wasn't a successful poker party.

✓ A Few Words About Priorities at Minnesota Poker Parties

If anybody needs a beer, the game stops until he gets it. And if nobody has heard the one about the one-legged Norwegian with priapism, the game stops. Of course, just about everybody has, but you can't hear a good story too many times. Nothing will offend a Minnesota poker player so much as interrupting a good story in order to play poker.

Remember: A poker party is an excuse to get out of the house. It might seem like the guys could just as well sit in the living room on soft chairs and tell the one about the hard-of-hearing old maid and the man from Roto-Rooter as many times as they wanted. But it wouldn't look right, would it? A bunch of guys just talking and drinking. You've got to have something to do while you're doing the other.

A fishing trip is in the same category as a poker party, except that trying to smoke, drink, and tell dirty stories in a rowboat while messing around with sharp objects is considerably more dangerous than poker played in a basement. If you ever get a hook in the side of your nose—which is one of the reasons I stopped drinking beer when I fish at night—you'll know what I mean. There is an occasional minor injury at a poker party—usually when somebody trips on food debris or pokes himself in the eye with a pretzel.

At a Minnesota poker party the noise never lets up—except during the 10 o'clock break when we all go watch the news. At the end of a hand the noise gets louder, because that's when the winner is attacked by everybody else and given a hard time. It's obligatory. Don't be afraid to join in.

But the real hubbub comes at the beginning of a hand when the new dealer (the deal rotates around the table) announces the game he wants to play. There will be a roar of confusion.

—"Didn't we just play that?"

—"I was shelling peanuts. Tell me again."

—"I don't understand."

—"What the hell kind of game is that?"

At a Minnesota poker party, nobody seems to know how to play anything anybody else does. The dealer sometimes doesn't even know how to play the game he's dealing. The talk is all part of the fun, the way it is in Monopoly. We like the games with a little meat to them. Simple five-card draw or seven-card stud are not very popular here—they just don't have enough rules or wild cards, and they don't require explanations. If you try playing only draw or stud at a poker party, the boys will head home early or fall asleep with their face in the chip dip.

—"Cut the cards. We're playing Midnight Minnetonka."

—"What? What did you say? Is that like Mud in Your Eye, where queens are wild unless a jack is turned up?"

—"No, you're thinkin' of Over the Hills and into the Woods, but you take out the deuces in Over the Hills and add the joker."

—"Huh? That's Sitting by the Side of the Road, isn't it? You get three cards, two down and one up. Then you bet, then you deal two in the middle that belong to everybody. That's the side road. But if one of the cards matches the card you got down, it's wild unless somebody raises."

—"That's Fast Freight. And nines and threes are wild."

—"That sounds like Pearl Harbor, to me. If a four is turned up, do you get to buy an extra card for a quarter?"

—"That's Chicken in a Basket, you bozo."

If the argument goes on too long the dealer will generally change his choice:

—"Okay, forget Midnight Minnetonka, the game is No Hunting or Trespassing."

—"Is that where you pass three cards to the left and then change chairs after the first bet?"

—"No. That's Mission Impossible."

—"Mission Impossible . . . Mission Impossible. Oh, yeah, I know that game. You deal out five cards, but you drop one of your cards over your left shoulder and if it lands face up, it's wild."

—"That's Fishing for Bullheads, and besides, it's the right shoulder."

But once we have the rules down, we get in the pot and stay there till the cows come home. After all, we came to play poker, not watch somebody else do it.

Bob Humde

AUTOMATIC LITTER BOX

Bob Humde here to tell you that the HUMDE SELF-DUMPING LITTER BOX is available at certain pet stores. I learned the hard way that a cat living inside the house doesn't always find the litter box. That's why I invented a litter box that finds the cat. When your cat starts scratching at the screen door or whimpering, the HUMDE LITTER BOX powers up and makes a beeline for the cat, wherever it is in the house. The rest is obvious. After several activations, the automatic litter box rolls outside and dumps itself behind the garage, and then refills itself with sand. In the testing phase, we thought cats might be scared of a moving litter box with blinking lights, but actually they developed an attachment to the HUMDE LITTER BOX and would scratch on the screen just to see it come wheeling up. After a week or two they would even take rides in it. It's pretty cute to see them riding around the house, jumping in and out. Your cats'll love it and you won't have to be picking up you-know-what and scrubbing your shag carpet.

Minnesota Body Language

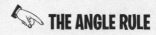 **THE ANGLE RULE**

Two standing Minnesotans never face each other during conversation. The angle made by the two intersecting lines running parallel to the chests of the participants should never be less than 45 degrees, 90 degrees is the average, 135 degrees is common, and 180 degrees is within reason. Heated arguments in public places would be in the 45-degree range. Voices are not raised.

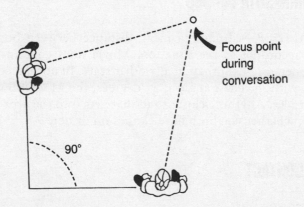

Focus point during conversation

90°

A simple discussion between two standing Minnesotans about the weather or the Twins' chances for getting out of the cellar would be conducted at a full 180 degrees—both would be staring off into the distance as they talked to each other.

If you are seated during conversation, the ideal angle can sometimes be achieved if you will move your chair. Two

Minnesotans in a living room for conversation will both sit on the sofa, one at each end, facing forward, with only an occasional side glance.

 EYE CONTACT

On subways in major American cities eye contact is avoided because it may be taken as a sign of weakness by the criminal element. We don't have any subways in Minnesota, but we avoid eye contact anyway. If a person looks directly at you and locks on to your eyes while he talks, we take that as a sign that he's selling something or not from around here, or both. If you are selling vacuum cleaners door to door in the Gopher State, don't talk too fast and don't lean over and get sincere by looking straight into the customer's eyes. There are ways to make a sale in Minnesota but that doesn't even come close.

 THE MINNESOTA MMDBB

The MMDBB—Minnesota mean distance between bodies— varies according to the situation. Movie lines contain fewer people per yard (.56) than in any other state. In normal conversation, with the chest angle at 45 degrees, the MMDBB would be four feet. Anything closer than that gets into the area of intimacy, whether you both have clothes on or not.

 BODY CONTACT

Keep your distance.

Avoid touching people.

Public body contact between Minnesotans is rare.

How much private body contact occurs in Minnesota is none of your business.

When you shake hands, get it over with fast and extend your arm the full length during the engagement. Don't ever reach over with your left hand and pat the other person's hand during the shake.

There is no "high-five" in Minnesota—it's called the "belt-five": the arms of the participants are fully extended at waist height and the palms and five fingers touch briefly.

In most situations where other people are in the vicinity, keep your arms folded or hanging straight down at your sides.

A recent computerized study of Minnesotan has shown that eighty-five words carry the load in Minnesota conversations. This core vocabulary was found to be smaller than that used by any discrete American group, except for the "B-Tens," a self-sufficient culture of bingo players in Los Angeles.

In a pioneering experiment at Prairie Gate College—conducted by psychology professor Clint ("Looking Out for Number 3 or 4") Beersford—a group of Minnesotans were hooked up to electrical wires during conversation in a laboratory setting and given a jolt every time they said *you bet* or *whatever.* In less than a day, all eight subjects were speechless.

Critics of the study said that if you put eight Minnesotans together for a day—in or out of the laboratory—they always end up speechless, and without being hooked up to electrical wires. I don't think there's any doubt about it.

Learning to talk Minnesotan is hard enough for visitors, but learning when not to talk is even tougher, I think. I wish I had all the answers for you on that. I don't know what to say.

And if that news is not bad enough, think of the fatal mistakes you can make with your nonverbal Minnesotan: Standing. Sitting. Walking. Gesturing. Raising your eyebrows. And the most difficult nonverbal art of the lot:

👉 WAVING IN MINNESOTA

More often than not, what brings the stranger to his knees here is waving. Waving—it looks like a simple act, but it's almost as complicated as spoken Minnesotan.

I remember my first wave. I was fifteen years old, driving a John Deere A—the one with the narrow front end and no self-starter. To start it you had to open the petcocks on the two cylinders to lower the compression and then spin the heavy flywheel by hand until the thing kicked over. That's the one I was on, just east of our farm there, going downhill. And coming up the hill was a guy in a car. I didn't recognize the car, but when it got closer, I could see it was Donny Goodman. He waved at me just before we passed, and I managed to get my arm in the air for a return wave. I didn't even think about it—I just did it. But I hit my thumb on the throttle lever coming up and I thought I could see a smirk on Donny's face.

It was a terrible wave. I dreamt about it. I'll never forget it. But now, more than thirty years later, I'm probably as good a waver as you'll find in Minnesota, but I still don't know it all, and if I'm tired, sometimes I'll even give the wrong wave in a situation.

Waving is a greeting delivered from a distance when one or both people are in some sort of motorized vehicle traveling in opposite directions. No waving situation develops when both people are out of their vehicles, because a wave involves the *passing process*, when one or both are *going by*.

However, when you meet somebody while you're out walking, a wave can be used to supplement the spoken word, but is never used by itself. (And for that matter, the classic wave from vehicle to vehicle *never* includes a verbal exchange. Rolling the driver's window down and saying something as you pass would be the height of folly. Even if you are both on open tractors with no cab, don't speak.)

If you meet and pass somebody walking, you should say "How's it going?" or "What'd'ya think of this weather then?" If you toss in a wave, make it a simple opening and closing of the hand. Any of the motorized waves would be overstaffing.

If a vehicle goes by your place while you're on the ground sawing down dead elms, walking beans, or changing the oil in the tractor, the responsibility for starting the wave process is yours. You look up or you don't. If you look up, you will wave if you know the person. On rare occasions you may wave at a perfect stranger going by if they look like they need a wave. This is the "goodwill" wave. The Minnesota Tourist Council ran a big billboard campaign on it a few years back, trying to get us to perform more goodwill waves. I think we're back to square one now, though.

A word about the "why me?" wave that does occur in some situations when both people are on the ground out of their vehicles and are standing still and see each other across a room or yard full of people holding plates of food. It usually happens at a family reunion, or a wedding, or some other place where you would rather be anyplace else than. This wave is delivered with the arm hanging at your side, the neutral position. The only motion is in the wrist—bring the fully opened hand up about 60 degrees and hold it a second and then slowly bring it down. This wave means, roughly: "I see you're about as miserable as I am in this deal."

Waving, by the way, takes place in the country, and in some smaller rural towns where everybody knows everybody else. But in the Twin Cities, or Duluth, or even Mankato and the other burgeoning urban centers of Minnesota, even people who know each other do not wave at each other. Maybe that's what's wrong with cities, I don't know. Neighbors in cities will sometimes wave at each other over their fences, as long as one of them doesn't have a dog that turns over garbage cans or yipes all night.

Another thing. Don't substitute honking for waving unless the other person just got married or you notice oats leaking from the truck where the rags fell out.

How Often to Wave

Never wave more than once if the same situation develops again in the same day. You wave twice at a person only if on the second time by they have either changed vehicles (bigger tractor, tractor to three-wheeler) or changed grains (hauling corn first time, beans second). If they've only taken off their jacket or changed seed corn hats, you should not wave again.

Sighting

Begin evaluating and identifying the approaching vehicle as far ahead as possible. It goes without saying that you should know what vehicles your friends and neighbors are currently driving and be able to recognize every single one of them from a distance. Once you are pretty sure you know who it is, get ready for the wave by easing up your grip on the steering wheel with your right hand. Even left-handers use their right for waves, don't ask me why. Clear a path for your arm: hitting the windshield or any other part of the vehicle or your own body during the wave is bad form. Also, do not lose control of your vehicle. If waving means you will risk driving into the ditch and out into the field, forget it. The other person will get over it in time.

When to Wave

If you are both in fast vehicles, the waving situation develops and is over before you can say "Boo," so wave when the vehicles are about ten yards apart. If you are both in slow vehicles— driving by the crops in the pickup or trying to find out where that turn is—the time to wave is pretty important, otherwise the *wave vacuum* can occur: the wave comes too soon and you are just passing each other without anything to do. If you wave too soon, it is best to check the pin on the wagon or find out what is under your foot. In fact, in slow vehicles, most drivers inspect their equipment right up until the passing moment.

Kinds of Waves

This is the tough part. The wave itself. It's so easy to foul up. It's almost better not to wave—or even honk the horn—than to use the wrong wave. Here are a few guidelines.

The ordinary garden-variety wave here is the finger wave. Your hand is gripping the steering wheel, you meet another vehicle, and you raise the index finger. You don't leave it up, you just flash it. The finger wave has more variations than I intend to go into here. Watch for it, try to imitate it.

The thumb is never featured in a wave.

Two- to four-finger waves are commonly used between fast-moving vehicles, but the nicely executed single-finger wave is a thing of beauty and a joy forever. To me, it perfectly sums up the Minnesota character that I love so much. The finger wave from the steering wheel: when you get it right, you'll know you've arrived and you don't ever have to leave again if you don't want to.

In general, if the situation for the wave is uncommon—say, if you or the other person has a gutted deer on the hood—then the wave should be a product of the imagination, but would certainly involve some horizontal movement of the whole arm.

A newcomer to Minnesota can't expect to do more than get the rudiments of waving down before crossing the border. Practice at home. Get a member of your family in a second vehicle and go by each other and wave. At least you'll have the mechanics of it down.

There is one Minnesota wave that doesn't come up all that much, once per person being the average. But you might as well be aware of it. Minnesota ranks very low among the states in production of famous last words, but we're high in production of last waves.

—"Did he say anything before he died?"

—"Nope. He just waved and then dropped his head on the pillow."

In this situation, the return wave is optional.

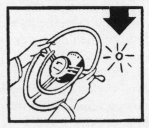

If your car has a lot of confusing gauges to look at, you need SMART LIGHT. The SMART LIGHT instrument panel is a complete blank and doesn't bother you with minor details like engine temperature or oil pressure. When something goes wrong, a simple sign flashes in red: "You're in Trouble." Just park your car and wait for the Smart Light Module to automatically dial the nearest certified SMART LIGHT mechanic.

Smart Light instrument panels:
one light, one warning.

There's not a simpler system made.

*The patented sleep device for
frequent travelers on bus and plane.*

JAWSLING fits over your head and supports your neck
and lower jaw. Simply attach the suction cup to the roof
and the cable to your JAWSLING head assembly and
you're ready to catch a few Zs without making a spectacle of yourself on public transportation.

"I'm a professional task-force facilitator and I fly a lot.
Before I purchased a JAWSLING it was difficult for me
to get comfortable enough to sleep, and of course, if I did
nod off, my mouth would fall open and I would drool
down the front of my sport jacket—that's when the flight
attendants would shake me awake. But that doesn't happen to me anymore, because I wear my JAWSLING. It
keeps my head from rolling around like a loose grape-
fruit and my mouth stays shut."

—D.M.L., Jackson Heights, N.Y.

*Why not carry an extra JAWSLING
for the stranger bobbing around next to you?*

*(JAWSLING also available with optional
SNORE & LURCH SUPPRESSOR.)*

Going up to the Lake and into the Lodge: An Update

Paradise

Driving up north in the summer to a lodge on one of Minnesota's fabled[1] ten thousand lakes has been a tradition for well over a century. Some of the first vacation lodges[2] rented to tourists and in-state adventurists toward the last decade of the nineteenth century and into the first decade of the twentieth could only be reached by boat and a lengthy trek with heavy canvas backpacks. The only amenities provided were a front door without a lock, a couple of windows, a wood-burning stove, a table, and cast iron cookware. The fishing was outstanding, nobody starved, and the arrival of a black bear or a wolf felt like a friendly welcome to the neighborhood. It was a somewhat safe education in survival for children and parents alike, a link to our American past, and tip of the hat to our ancestors for being so tough. Children young and old were in hog heaven in these lodges.

That sort of back-to-the-land tourism is still being approximated in the Boundary Waters of northeastern Minnesota in 2012: canoeing, portages, camping in tents, cooking over open fires, and yes, a welcome[3] to the neighborhood from the odd wolf, black bear, or cougar.

Paradise Relaxed

By 1987, when *How to Talk Minnesotan* was published, fishing lodges in Minnesota continued to be extremely popular for visitors seeking a little peace and quiet and a chance for total relaxation. Walleyes were caught and fried fresh less than an hour from the

---

[1] "Fabled" not because there aren't that many, but because there are several thousand more than that, and not even Google knows how many for sure.

[2] "Shacks" would better describe these accommodations.

[3] Wolves, bears, and cougars are smart creatures. I could believe them capable of sarcasm. I personally think they are sick of us.

water. Visitors went swimming or water skiing. They periodically fired up the rental boat for a "Sunday drive" around the lakeshore to look at the other lodges and the many second homes of Minnesotans and the huge summer homes of the sort of rich and sort of famous. They took naps whenever they felt like it. They read the books they brought from the library back home. They told stories around the campfire on the beach. The guys ambled up to lodge headquarters where they talked to the manager about life in the Northwoods, maybe tipping a brew with the other guests, many of whom were summer friends, because they too had been coming there forever it seemed. Over the years families became sentimentally attached to a particular lodge and even a particular cabin. Not going back every year to Cabin 7 would have been a sacrilege, especially so since somewhere along the way three generations had begun to make the northern trek, with Cabins 5 and 6 now part of the tradition.

Paradise Lost

I am not sure when the dam burst, but when I was up at the lake one year, probably 1998, a guy carrying a laptop was asking the lodge manager when he was going to get an Internet connection and how did he expect him to be out of touch with his office for so long. Nothing came of it and that guy never returned. We already had spotty cell service, and I for one thought spotty was quite enough, but the next year a cell phone tower rose blinking above the trees.

And then all of a sudden new lodges and old in Minnesota started advertising broadband Wi-Fi, flat-screen TV with 120 cable channels, and DVD players, and with it came a host of Jet skis whipping around the lake. It was so loud some days, as my mother liked to say, you couldn't hear yourself think. Air-conditioning became standard for lodges. The families arrived not in one car but in three or four SUVs that blocked views to the shore. Nobody seemed to be fishing much. Teenagers sat around looking at their smartphone screens, using the word *boring* like a punch in the nose. Nobody brought books, because like most Americans they got what they needed from TV. Cars were coming and going all day and into the night.

Personally, I could sleep easier at my sister's house in St. Paul near the freeway than I could at our old lodge, which no longer exists you should know, sold to a developer and bulldozed to make condos.

Rebuilding Paradise

Harold Mire's second cousin Sidney built the first ecolodge on Lake Winnibigoshish in 2010. He advertises no phone service except by using the lodge's phone. No air-conditioning, no TV. The boats are all powered by oars. Guests fish from rowboats, no fish-finders allowed, and no microwaves—too dangerous according to Sidney's dad, who was a radar operator in the Korean War, where they used to roast chickens with the radar in less than three minutes as long as there were no incoming targets. He assumed Sidney would not like his guests to be roasted to perfection by some poorly wired microwaves.

CREAKING CABIN LODGE on Leech Lake was a mom-and-pop establishment on the verge of being sold, cabins and all, in 2009 by the owners Marvin and Trish. At their age they could go back to farming a few acres and having Marvin drive the school bus. They would have Social Security to help, but they had no health insurance except Medicare. CREAKING CABIN LODGE never did have a whole lot of amenities, and when the other cabins on Leech Lake put in Wi-Fi, Marv and Trish did not own a computer or quite understand the fascination of the Internet. Besides they could not afford putting it in even if they had wanted to, which they didn't.

Marvin and Trish decided to hold out one more season: if the bookings were good, they would hang in there. Their granddaughter Cathy, who had an advertising degree from the U, said she would do their advertising. She set up a website for CREAKING CABIN LODGE with a counterintuitive (her words) campaign. No air-conditioning, lots of fans though, no Jet Skis, no flat- or round- or square-screen TVs. No DVD player. No cell phone service. Emergency calls on the lodge phone were free, if it was working. The sagging mattresses were as welcome as ever and the rusty water out of the faucet was considered a health tonic. "What we guarantee is good walleye fishing and a week of peace and quiet, at a pace and price your grandparents always enjoyed."

Marvin and Trish filled all the cabins for the summer and into September, because the old customers were coming back and the new ones were bringing their children so they could enjoy a return to nature and some good fried walleye.

In early 2012 some of the highly digitized lodges were filing for bankruptcy, with ever-declining reservations and increased media bills. As reported in the papers, their customers cancelled because they saw no reason to go north when they had everything they needed back home in the way of smartphones, flat HDTV, streaming movies, Facebook, and Twitter.

Directions

 ASKING DIRECTIONS

If you need directions on a motoring tour through rural Minnesota, simply stop the car when you see a Minnesotan and speak through your rolled-down driver's window. If the directions get involved—which is very likely—you can get out and stretch your legs. Nearly 50 percent of Minnesota conversations are conducted through the side window of a car or pickup or while leaning on the fender or hood, 30 percent are conducted over a little lunch at the kitchen table, 15 percent in a rowboat, and the remaining 5 percent take place in movie theaters during the movie. According to a recent study.

Words and Phrases

✓ *I think I took a wrong turn.*

✓ *Howda ya git ta?*

✓ *Run that by me again, would you?*

Dialogue Practice

DRIVER: "Say, howda ya git ta the Anderson farm? I think we took a wrong turn."

MINNESOTAN: "I figured something was up—this is your fourth time by and the sightseeing ain't the greatest here, unless you count my brother-in-law, but he don't get out much. Which way'd you come in?"

D: "From the north, I think. We went by this house with old tires in the front yard and the windows boarded up. It looked like it'd been struck by a high wind."

M: "It was, in '79. Some people said it was a tornado. That's where I live. I been meanin' to fix it up. So it wasn't north—you came in from the south."

D: "Does it matter?"

M: "Not to me it don't. But if you want to get where you're going, it does. Did you see the elevator?"

[*Note*: This is the *grain elevator*, which is several stories taller than everything else in small towns except maybe the water tower. It's where corn, soybeans, oats, and wheat are elevated and stored until they are shipped out in boxcars or trucks, and it's where all directions start. —H.M.]

M: "Okay, so, you go past the elevator then, on the blacktop. There is a gravel road there, but don't take it, take the blacktop until it comes to a tee where the welding shop used to be. It's just a field now. I think it's got corn in it this year. Ya go left there. You could go right there, but it'd be longer. A lot of people go that way, but I wouldn't. Ya go left then for, oh, say, I don't know, half a mile, three-quarters, maybe. It's just before the road dips where the sewage lagoon flooded last fall. You can't miss it. You take a left and go past the Pepper place— nobody lives there now. Past the big grove of dead elms. The next place is the Anderson farm, that's Orv Anderson. He married the oldest Peterson girl. That's Pete Peterson. Not Jack Peterson. He never had any kids, Jack didn't. The place after that is *Arnie* Anderson's. Orv and Arnie are brothers. Sven was their father. But if you're looking for the Olaf Andersons, then that's another matter. Remember the elevator? Well, take that gravel road south around Dead Gopher Lake. You can't miss it."

D: "Run that by me again, would you?"

M: "Why don't I just draw you a map then?"

Here's what the map will look like, only it'll be in pencil on part of a grocery bag or the inside of a cigarette pack:

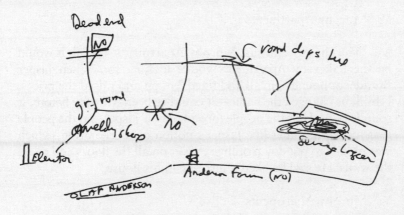

Saying "Run that by me again" to a Minnesotan who has just given you directions goes without saying, because all directions will be given at least twice—three times is the average. No way to get around it, stay where you are and listen. It could be that he wasn't completely sure how to get to where you wanted to go but told you anyway to the best of his knowledge and then got more confident as he talked. By the second or third version he'll be as confident as you are about how accurate he is. (Myself, when I give directions I remember things I didn't know I knew. And frankly, telling people how to get to where they want to go is something I always do gladly. It's as selfless as turning off somebody's headlights in a parking lot.)

VISITOR: "How do you get to the Murphy Apartments?"

MINNESOTAN: "Murphy Apartments. Murphy Apartments. Murphy Apartments. They used to call 'em the Lakeview Apartments. Does that sound right to you?"

V: "I don't know. It's a woman I used to go to school with lives there, she's from Illinois, which is where I'm from. She said Murphy Apartments. I thought it'd be easy to find."

M: "You'd think so, wouldn't you then? Illinois, huh? You're a long way from home."

V: "Murphy Apartments . . ."

M: "Murphy Apartments. Murphy Apartments. I think it would be the Lakeview Apartments you're looking for. When Jasper Brandenot bought 'em all and fixed 'em up and raised the prices, I think he changed the name—it could've been Murphy before. It sounds right. Half the people moved out on Jasper and the people that moved in didn't like Jasper's notion of redecoration, which was mainly to put down orange carpet on all the floors and panel the walls. He said he liked it just fine in his house."

V: "Murphy Apartments . . ."

M: "Lakeview, that's where you're headed. They used to be the Murphy Apartments. Sure. See that radio tower way off over there? Go down this street to the stop sign, turn left and go up that hill past the radio tower and then you'll see the Armory on the right and the Avon headquarters on the left. Go another hundred feet or so, you can't miss it."

V: "Thanks. I've got it."

M: "Yep, you just go to the stop sign and head for the radio tower. The Avon regional manager lives there. She's quite the lady. Sometimes you can smell perfume when you drive by, especially on delivery day. That's it, all right."

V: "Well, I appreciate it."

Bob Humde

BARKING PEN

Bob Humde here for my rechargeable BARK-ING PEN. If you lose a BOB HUMDE BARK-ING PEN or somebody steals it, you just let out a bark, and the pen will bark back and you can find it. The BOB HUMDE BARK-ING PEN also barks when you click the top to write with it. You can use it to scare off intruders, or give yourself more room on a bus. But don't click it around dogs—they'll tear your clothes off.

M: "You bet. Just go up here to the stop sign and head for the radio tower, until you smell perfume, and then you'll see the Lakeview Apartments—the old Murphy Apartments. They thought about starting a college in that neighborhood and those apartments were gonna be dormitories, they said. I don't what happened to that idea."

At this point, you should be in your car and moving. Give a little open palm wave as you drive off.

FLYING MINNESOTAN: AN UPDATE

It was not long after *How to Talk Minnesotan* was published in 1987 that I started getting letters from out-of-state pilots as far away as New Jersey, and Florida, and even Canada, informing me that they did not drive to the lodges. They flew in their own planes, some of which were float planes that could land on the lake and dock next to their fishing boats close to the lodge. What they mostly told me was how useful they found *How to Talk Minnesotan* for flying in. After three or four years of flying into Minnesota they were, they said, finally beginning to talk flying Minnesotan like a pro.

The Immersion Method for Out-of-State Pilots (Not Recommended)

Here's a pretty dramatic letter dated 2007 from a private pilot, John, from Austin, Texas:

> My first time comin' to Minnesota, back around July 1990, I had no trouble along the way talkin' to air traffic controllers in Oklahoma, or Missouri, or Kansas. I could even understand Iowans, but Holy Smokes, when I crossed the border headed for the Duluth area, I can fess up without the FAA fining me retroactively. I could not understand a lot of what the air traffic controllers wanted me to do. You gotta know that can be kinda dangerous when you're fixin' to land, or takin' off. What happened is, I missed the part where Duluth tower said two F-16s were on long final for runway 9. But a few seconds later I heard it clearly when tower yelled it. Yelling I understand, including all the other words tower used instead of my name. I had already seen the Air Guard F-16s coming in hot and was not about to get in their way. "It was not a good deal" is what I can say today because we have been coming to Minnesota every summer since and I can talk the lingo and hear it, "you bet." I wish I had known about *How to Talk Minnesotan* on my first flight to Minnesota.

A Few Words About Minnesota's Rural Grass Strips

Quite a few Minnesotans own their own planes, and normally hangar them at a local airport, where maintenance is conducted by certified airframe and power plant mechanics. But the truth is that plenty of farmers have an older single engine Cessna or Piper, mainly hangared in a barn or shed near the self-made grass strip, which is rarely longer than 2000 feet, plenty of runway for a Piper Warrior or a Cessna 150. It would be safe to say, or maybe unsafe to say, that birds invariably get into the improvised hangars and do what comes naturally. The favorite site for bird nests is the air intake for the engine. It is widely understood that an internal combustion engine needs air to mix with the gas in order for the propeller to turn at the appropriate speed.

The flying farmers pull the plane out of the barn (hangar) with the tractor or four-wheeler ATV. The next step is to check the fuel, oil, and all the other items on the official checklist, if you can find the checklist. Kick the tires. Search and remove bird nests if it has been a few months since the last flight, or it's the first flight after the winter snow melts off the grass strip. Crank her up, check the mags, and put on the headset and do a radio check in case a mouse or two has munched on the wiring. Since it is a private strip, you test the radios by calling your wife or whoever in the house has the handheld transceiver. There is always a chance that other pilots farther away will hear you on the common frequency.

PILOT: "Okay, then, it's me, can you hear me, Sally?"

SALLY: "Yes, honey, I can hear you. Did you remember to take the sandwiches?"

MALE VOICE: "We read you loud and clear, honey. We're at 30,000 feet in a 737, heading for Detroit. Have a good day!"

PILOT: "I'm in a Cessna 150 ready to depart from my farm, heading for Appleton, Minnesota, climbing to 3000 feet. I see your contrail, 737."

Rules and Regulations

For the farmer, or anybody else with a private strip who wants to fly his plane, the basic legal requirements are a pilot's certificate and a current FAA medical, but it would not be too far-fetched to think that farmer pilots and other rural pilots might be cutting a corner or two.

I wouldn't want to be questioned too closely about whether I know any World War II pilots who might be stretching the FAA rules. A good friend of mine was a B-24 engineer in the 307th Bombardment Group. He survived fifty bomb runs from a strip on an island in the South Seas and made it home in one piece, sort of. He loved flying his Piper Archer off the grass strip on his son's farm north of town. A great guy, gentle, easy-going, and I can tell you all this because he has been out of reach of the FAA (I hope they don't have that kind of reach) for four years. I do miss him. He was a natural pilot, who had learned to fly when he was seventeen, a year before the military snapped him up for the Pacific Theater.

In his later years Bud did not have a medical from the FAA, and no official pilot's certificate, though he did every four or five years go up with a young instructor who put him through the paces for a checkride, picking up a few good flying tips himself from Bud.

Bud was well-known at the little airports and grass strips where he landed to do some hangar flying, the pilot's term for drinking bad coffee and exchanging aviation stories. Bud was never ramp checked by the FAA, a pretty good streak of luck, really.

One time in early 1982, Bud got a phone call at home out of the blue and the guy on the other end said, "Is this my engineer I'm talking to?" It was Bud's pilot. He had not heard his voice for thirty-six years, but it seemed like yesterday.

I Don't Know

I don't know as used in Minnesota can have the same meaning as *I don't know* elsewhere in the nation—that is, it can mean that the speaker doesn't know something.

—"Honey, where's the spring that goes inside the roller for the toilet paper holder?"

—"I don't know."

—"You took it out and then you put the roll on top of the toilet tank. How could somebody just lose the spring?"

—"I don't know."

—"How do you figure you can function in the real world with an attitude like that?"

—"I don't know."

However, the more common use of *I don't know* in Minnesota is to hang it at the end of a sentence—or rarely, at the beginning—as a kind of verbal shrug of resignation. In this case it doesn't mean you don't know, it means you do know but you're not going into detail for some reason, usually because you've said too much already, or implied it.

A: "I never saw two more unlikely people to be dating than Craig and the Swenson girl, I don't know."

B: "They say they're gonna get married. I don't know."

A: "The Swensons are nice enough, nothing you could really fault 'em for, but those kids of theirs, sometimes I don't know."

B: "Yeah, sometimes a guy just don't know, you know."

After a conversation of that sort, you end up knowing something, not that it's a whole lot of consolation. But in some cases you don't know even when you clearly do know.

—"I took algebra, I took calculus, I took computer studies. And here I am running a backhoe. I don't know."

🖝 FURTHER PRACTICE

Here's a Minnesotan reporting on the condition of his new car:

—"Barely 5,000 miles on it, and there's oil dripping down off the crankcase. I don't know."

(Among other things you don't know in this statement is how come they can't build a car that'll run a ways before it breaks down and starts dripping oil, which your '49 Ford did not do until it turned over a 100,000, and then the gasket only cost you seventy-five cents and the garage put it in for five bucks. But although you don't know, you do know. You know you're gonna have to pull the valve cover and put in a new gasket, and the way they build engines these days you're gonna have to take off a hundred hoses and who knows what else. Just to stop an oil drip.)

A farmer during spring planting:

A: "You get a couple of dry days, and you get the planter in the field and then it rains. I don't know."

B: "It's bad enough dealing with the banks, but the weather, I don't know."

A: "They say it balances out, but I don't know."

Of course he knows: it balances out, but that does not mean that you will ever get a perfect spring or a bank that won't patronize. Somebody will, but not you.

Reading the newspaper:

—"Look at this story. I don't know."

(Sure you know: You don't know what this world is coming to.)

I don't know, like so many Minnesota phrase workhorses, is used to keep from saying too much. It puts the burden on the listener. If you want to know more, if you need elaboration, you have to ask, otherwise your guess is as good as anybody's. (Unless of course you have asked a Minnesotan for directions or wonder what he's driving—then you'll get all the elaboration you need, and a little more.)

In a Minnesota conversation, the implication of an opinion is enough. The exact opinion is hardly ever called for, or is understood in a general sort of way.

Take politics:

—"Did you see who decided to run for governor? I don't know."

—"Isn't that always the way it is?"

—"You got that right."

From the Desk of the President of the Minnesota Tourist Council: A Message About Hankies

Whenever I leave home I carry a clean hanky because you never know when a tourist might be watching you. And nothing makes a bigger impression than a clean hanky. So let's all do our part, especially during the flu and cold season when hankies really get a workout. Myself, I take a clean hanky from my dresser drawer every morning and fold it into a neat square and slip it into my back pocket. When I need to use it, I unfold it discreetly and make a little pocket in it for my nose and conduct my business. Don't ever jerk the hanky out of your pocket and wave it around. And please watch the decibel level.

Here are some other hanky tips. It's okay to use a hanky to dab at your brow or take care of your sweaty palms. But don't polish your shoes with your hanky, don't use it to wipe up food spills off restaurant floors, don't drape your hanky over your shoulder when you burp babies, and don't carry your bait in it when you go fishing. And yes, I know it's a temptation to keep the same hanky in your pocket for weeks and weeks, but it won't make our tourists feel welcome.

And while you're at it, maybe carry two hankies. One for yourself and one for a tourist—just in case.

My name is
Norman Ackbom

My name is Norman Ackbom and I was out the other day in my old flat-bottomed boat fishing for bluegills and listening to a Twins game on my transistor radio and I thought—what the heck—I don't have much of anything else to do, I'm gonna run for governor of Minnesota.

If you vote for me, I pledge to work toward keeping things pretty much as they are. If there's something that seems to need something, I'll look into it, but otherwise I don't see any point in rocking the boat.

So then, in closing, if you make me your governor you won't get any big surprises thrown at you, that's all I can say.

NORMAN H. ACKBOM
FOR GOVERNOR
OF MINNESOTA

[The preceding political announcement was written and paid for by Norman Ackbom in his own behalf.]

(Adv.)

CELL PHONE RECOVERY

CELL PHONE RECOVERY is a company dedicated to finding and reconditioning cell phones for the economy market. With over fifteen employees in Minnesota and twelve employees in adjacent states, CELL PHONE RECOVERY is a niche company whose job is to save the environment by recycling lost or destroyed cell phones from unusual locations. Company CEO Ackley Drust fondly remembers that summer day in 2010 when he got the idea for his company while in a foursome on a Minnetonka golf course, where he was about to putt an easy five footer, when his brother-in-law's cell phone played taps. "Give me that d____ thing!" he said. Ackley grabbed the phone, dropped it to the ground, took out his driver, and whacked the phone seventy yards into the large water hazard near the twelfth hole. The way Ackley tells it everybody was real quiet and then Ackley said, "I wonder how many cell phones are in the water hazards on this course?" He did not have to wonder long, because the divers he hired found fifty-three cell phones with all manner of what appeared to be golf club impact marks, though many were undamaged except for being waterlogged and were apparently simply lobbed into the lake for reasons only a golfer would know.

Ackley also likes to tell the story about the morning he accidentally flushed his cell phone down the toilet and wondered just how many cell phones a day suffered that fate. CELL PHONE RECOVERY bought exclusive rights to that cell phone gold mine. In the Twin Cities metro area alone, Ackley's dedicated employees rescued over 225 cell phones caught in sewage plant filters, all of which have already been reconditioned and sold at selected retail outlets in Minnesota, including a kiosk in the Mall of America.

According to Ackley, his company is growing fast. Cell phones by the thousands will eventually be reclaimed daily, refurbished, and placed in the hands of customers who want a cheap cell phone that helps save the environment from untold contamination. All refurbished phones are pasteurized.

Find CELL PHONE RECOVERY on Facebook and read more heart-warming stories about Ackley's entrepreneurial spirit and read the testimonies of satisfied customers. Gordy is currently hiring associates to cover the growing population of cell phone users and losers in the oil fracking territory of western North Dakota.

Lesson 26

Lists, the Phone, For Sure, Saying Too Much

 ### USING THE PHONE IN MINNESOTA

As you should know by now, the heartbeat of conversation in Minnesota is the pause. If you don't get that right, you won't fool anybody except yourself. Just when you think we're through talking, we get going again. By radical comparison, take New York cab drivers. If you say "Boy, the federal government, I wonder sometimes" to a New York cabbie outside St. Patrick's Cathedral—which I did, the time I was in New York— you won't have to say another word until you get to Kennedy Airport. I didn't have anything else to say anyway. That same remark to a Minneapolis cabbie resulted in

—"Yeah, you bet."

But I've drifted from the subject. What follows is a typical phone conversation in Minnesota. I have indicated pauses where they naturally occur. You can try this at home before your visit here, but make sure the other party knows what you're up to, or they'll think they've been disconnected or there's trouble on your line. Frankly, when I make phone calls to strangers in other states (mostly catalog phone orders) I make an effort to reply as fast as I can because I get tired of hearing "Are you there?" or "Are you okay, sir?" It seems like New Jersey is the worst.

Here's the conversation. It's one I had once. The person I dialed is called X because he had no interest in being in this book or any other. I don't either but I don't have any choice.

Use it as a model. At first you should repeat it as written, but later you can develop your own subjects and force them into the basic framework. Maybe you can think of more interesting subjects. But interest is not my aim here—I'm just trying to help you survive. Making things interesting is mostly up to you. We're not running an amusement park in Minnesota. If you want to be amused, go to Las Vegas or Disneyland.

X: "Yep."

HM: "Is that you?"

[*Pause*]

X: "Who else would it be?"

[*Pause*]

HM: "I was gonna bring that kitchen table over tonight. I got her sanded."

[*Pause*]

X: [X did not reply here because it was obvious.]

HM: "I'd say it'd be a half hour."

[*Pause*]

X: "I'll be here."

[*Pause*]

HM: "I'm not saying it wouldn't be three-quarters of an hour."

X: "No problem."

HM: "Well."

X: "Yep."

HM: "So okay then. I'll drive on over pretty soon."

X: "Good deal."

HM: "All right, I'll get her loaded."

A word about wrong numbers in Minnesota. You know how it is, if you call a wrong number you feel like you stepped in something fresh. In Minnesota we believe a person is miserable enough without blaming them for the mistake. Here's the full text of my conversation with a guy who called my number by mistake.

X: "Ernie?"

HM: "No, this is Harold." [I never use my real name on the phone. You never know.]

X: "Is this 5263?"

HM: "I'm sorry, this is 4265. What did you want Ernie for?"

X: "My Plymouth—it's a '79 V-8—it's making a hissing noise. Ernie's real good with Plymouths."

HM: "I'm not too bad myself. Is there a kind of dull clicking with it?"

X: "Not really."

HM: "I'd say power brake vacuum booster."

X: "I appreciate it."

HM: "No problem. If you need any more help, give me a ring. You remember the wrong number, don't you?"

From the President's Desk of the Minnesota Tourist Council: a Message About Front Yards

As soon as the snow melts in May, I always make a point of going around with the wheelbarrow and picking up the dead animals and fruit rinds out of my front yard, because you never know when a tourist might drive by. In the winter nothing is more natural than throwing stuff out the front door into the yard, because it disappears under the snow. But in our two hot months, steak gristle, mayonnaise jars, and mounds of leftover broccoli-tuna hotdish can create an ugly, smelly mess. I'm not talking about the rusty cars and old washing machines—a guy's got to have someplace to store that junk. But come on, folks, do your part for Minnesota and get that rotten stuff out of your front yard in May. I know it's easy to let it go and just say, well, in a couple of months it'll be snowing again, but right now, let's face it, it's not going to make our tourists feel welcome. And while you're at it, maybe work on the backyard, too, just in case a visitor looks over the fence.

 **FOR SURE**

For sure in Minnesota is in the ballpark with *I don't know.* You can say "I don't know" and mean that you do know but you aren't saying how much you do know, or more rarely, that you actually don't know. The same goes for *for sure*, which mainly means that you are not sure, but you are saying you are sure in order to avoid a disagreement, or you just plain want to get through a murky area of the conversation.

You bet—by comparison—is usually a more positive statement of agreement. *For sure* or even *You got that right* both express reservations without going into detail. That's not to say that *you bet* can't be used to divert opinion—for example, where a citizen on a high horse says

> —"They oughta throw the book at 'em, sell their property, and give 'em a one-way ticket out of here."

> —"You bet."

That *you bet* does not mean you bet, it probably means you don't bet but are saying you do. On the other hand, it could also be taken as an all-purpose *you bet* that means: *You and I are talking, we are here, it's a short life, let's keep it calm, what's the sense of stirring up trouble? You got that right* as a reply is a stronger commitment to the incensed citizen's point of view: it could lead to elaboration on his part.

A FURTHER WORD ABOUT SAYING TOO MUCH

Rattling on and on is bad enough in Minnesota, but combining it with erratic gesturing and body movement could put a damper on your vacation. If you're a visitor from the Big Apple, say, and are in the Big Soybean for the first time, think before you talk, and then cut what you were planning to say by 90 percent. If in doubt, don't say anything.

In other words, don't tell your life story every time somebody asks you a simple question. There are married couples in Minnesota who have lived together for sixty years who do not know each other's life stories. If you persist in telling a Minnesotan way more than he wants to know (which is way less than you think he wants to know), you might as well repack your bags and buy a return ticket—your vacation is on its last legs.

HOW MUCH IS TOO MUCH?

It's hard to say. Take the world of Minnesota politics. When running for any office, big or small, you should avoid sounding like you have a platform. You should sound like you only have a plank or a five-gallon pail to stand on.

Right answers are never long answers.

In Boxelder, Minnesota, four candidates for the open spot on the school board answered this question: What changes in the school would you work for if elected? (Reprinted from the *Boxelder Bugle*, May 1985.)

Candidate #1: I don't know. I'd have to think about it.

Candidate #2: Well, that's a good question.

Candidate #3: None, I guess. Things haven't been too bad so far.

Candidate #4: We've got to have more communication between administrators and the parents, and between the teachers and the parents. What would be wrong with starting a PTA? I believe the community should get more involved in how the school is run. It's our school, after all.

Which candidate won the election?

#1 got 432 votes.

#2 got 287 votes (she shouldn't have said it was a good question).

#3 got 103 votes (made the mistake of implying that there was room for improvement with the *I guess*).

#4 got 12 votes (eleven relatives and self; eight other relatives, including his wife, voted for #1 and said so publicly).

Enough said.

EXCERPTS FROM
The Minnesota Book of Lists

(Reprinted by permission of the publisher.)

The Top Fifteen Opening Gambits in Minnesota Conversation

1. The heat's not bad if you don't move around.
2. I notice they're tearing up Twelfth Street for some reason.
3. I never thought I'd say this last February, but I'm sort of looking forward to winter now.
4. I never thought I'd say this last August, but I'm sort of looking forward to summer now.
5. Has anybody ever said you look like Walter Mondale?
6. Been having pretty good luck with that car?
7. Do you think it really helps to burp the Tupperware lid?
8. How much rain did you get? My gauge showed an inch.
9. Were you listening to WCCO this morning?
10. The Twins are struggling now.
11. Looks like it's shaping up to be a pretty nice day.
12. Have you been to Canterbury Downs yet?
13. To be honest, I never thought they'd get that Ice Palace built.
14. This is funny weather, isn't it?
15. They said it wasn't a tornado, but if it wasn't, I don't know what it was.

Four Knickknacks Found on Every Minnesota Whatnot Shelf

1. Miniature wicker cat.
2. Souvenir spoon from St. Paul Polka Daze.
3. Shiny rock from the backyard.
4. Salt and pepper shakers shaped like grain elevators.

A List of the All-Time Five Top-Selling Books in Minnesota

1. *Oversize Zucchini: A Guide to Painful Weight Loss*, by Art Nelson, as told to Vera Quirk, his personal physician.

2. *Boy, It Makes You Wonder Sometimes*, the memoirs of Floyd Yeakley, the father of the NoTug Milking Harness.
3. *Loose Bales, Dead Groundhogs, Funny Stripes on the Trees*, poems by A. V. Hind, three-time winner of the coveted Governor's Medallion for Poetry About Livestock.
4. *Consumer's Directory of Pretty Good Deals on Things You Might Not Buy Otherwise.*
5. *Stop and Go*, by Dorey Burt, a first novel about driving to work every day.

The Three Biggest Commercial Flops in Minnesota

1. Tofu on a stick.
2. Colored shirts.
3. The 11 o'clock news.

A List of Things Said to Customers in Minnesota Food Co-Ops

1. You're supposed to bring your own bags.
2. That's peanut butter—what did you think it was?
3. It's got sludge in the bottom of the jar because it's 100 percent natural.
4. Those are edible sweatbands.

The Sweet Corn Institute

When the sweet corn starts coming in strong in the home gardens, it's usually ready when you're not—but it has to be put up and laid by, there's no sense in wasting it. How is sweet corn best preserved? Most people freeze it. And here are some suggested tried-and-true methods from veteran sweet-corn freezers.

1. Shuck the ears, boil the ears, cut the kernels off, soak in cold water, and freeze immediately in bags.

2. Shuck the ears, but don't boil the ears, cut the kernels off raw, soak in hot water, and freeze hot.

3. Blanch the corn on the cob, silks and all, cool the whole cob, freeze it on the cob wrapped in newspapers.

4. Cook the cobs till the kernels are mushy and fall off. Cream the corn and freeze it hot in bags.

5. Cut the whole stalk down at ground level and boil everything until the shucks and silks fall off, then freeze the stuff that floats.

6. Cut the corn off raw and add a cup of whisky to each gallon of corn, heat to lukewarm, freeze with a maraschino cherry.

7. Go over your sweet-corn patch with the lawn mower, rake away the green part, freeze the yellow part.

8. Buy canned corn in the store, open the cans, dump the contents into freezer containers, label them with the date and your name.

WALLEYE PHONE
COMPANY
of Minnesota

(A Sustaining Sponsor of This Guide)

[Note: I am a charter subscriber at WALLEYE PHONE. My phone bill was seventy or eighty dollars a month before I signed on with Walleye. Now it runs about eight dollars and I'm not just saying that. The following phone interview with owner-operator Howie Humde is reprinted courtesy of *LongSpeak*, the national organ for alternative phone services. —H.M.]

LongSpeak: "Can you hear me, Howie? There's an echo in the line."

Howie Humde: "It's been doing that. You're lucky you got through."

LS: "WALLEYE PHONE is a new company, isn't that right?"

HH: "Yes, sir, we threw our hat into the Minnesota telecommunications ring almost a year ago."

LS: "Just to get a general idea, Howie, what does it cost a WALLEYE customer to make a three-minute call to Chicago?"

HH: "Not a cent. But it's not on our list. Not too many of our customers know people in Chicago anyway. At present we offer long-distance service to ten major cities in Minnesota, including southwest Duluth, Maynard, and Hanley Falls—in Hanley there, it's only east of the tracks because we couldn't get a clearance to dig under the Burlington Northern."

LS: "What other states can your customers call?"

HH: "None, as of yet. We can't do everything at once. Minnesota first, that's our motto."

LS: "But didn't WALLEYE PHONE recently put up a satellite? That must've helped a lot."

HH: "Not as much as we thought. It was an older model we picked up for a song and we didn't get the orbit quite right. It's too low and makes a high-pitched whistling noise when it sails by. It's basically a dud. We're gonna shoot her down and look for a newer one."

LS: "What special services do you offer at WALLEYE PHONE?"

HH: "All our customers get unlisted phone numbers free of charge. We don't publish a directory and we don't have directory service."

LS: "That's innovative, Howie. As you probably know, the in-car phones are very popular right now. Can your customers make important business calls while driving to work?"

HH: "No problem. As long as they take north-south roads and stay on high ground and don't go faster than about fifteen. Reception's been spotty in the Fords."

LS: "Let's straighten this out for our readers, Howie. Anybody in St. Paul can have a WALLEYE phone in their home and call anybody in ten major cities. Is that right?"

HH: "Absolutely. As long as they call between 9:30 in the morning, when Gertie throws the switch, and 3:30 in the afternoon, when she goes home to miss the traffic. We plan to be a twenty-four-hour phone company a couple of years down the road. It's in the master plan."

LS: "I hate to bring this up, Howie, but I really don't understand how you can compete with companies like AT&T. As you know, they say in their advertisements that you can call anybody in the world, any time."

HH: "Typical. What they don't say in those ads is that everybody in the world can call you, too. We don't even install two-way service unless people ask for it. Most of our customers, if they want any reaching out and touching done, they're gonna do it themselves."

LS: "Howie, if people want to sign up with WALLEYE PHONE, should they give you a call there at your office?"

HH: "Not really. We're having a few technical problems with this line. Their best bet would be to write me a letter and I'll send a guy out."

LS: "Thanks, Howie, for consenting to talk to us. You're fading, Howie. Any one last thing you want to say?"

HH: "We're cheap and we're friendly at WALLEYE PHONE. What more could you ask for?"

The Minnesota Long Good-bye

If you say hello during your visit to Minnesota, you'll probably say good-bye at some point. The Minnesota greeting may seem a little on the slim side to you, but don't worry—we make up for it when we say good-bye. The clearest measure of affection in Minnesota is the Long Good-bye. Saying good-bye is our strong suit.

Phrases

✓ *We better head out.*
✓ *It's getting late.*
✓ *It's past my bedtime.*
✓ *Let's hit the road.*

The most important thing to remember in the execution of a Minnesota Long Good-bye is to begin early, long before you actually climb in your car. The preparatory statement should be directed to your spouse—or to yourself if you're visiting alone; the people you are leaving will overhear it.

In the first stage of departure, never speak directly to those you are leaving. (Speaking indirectly will serve you well in other areas during your visit. See *Indirectness* elsewhere in this guide.)

Dialogue

(These guests have spent the day with their Minnesota hosts, evening has fallen, supper is over.)

—"Well, Doris, I suppose we oughta hit the road."

—"You bet, honey. It's about that time."

—"You two just got here. Stay awhile. Did we do something wrong?"

You will be offered another cup of coffee and a light lunch. Go ahead and eat, let your food settle, then with a halfhearted lunge from your seat and a yawn, speak directly to your host:

—"It's past our bedtime. We really gotta go."

—"Are you kidding? The news just started."

Watch the 10 o'clock news at least through the weather forecast.

—"Well, this is it, we're leaving."

—"Why don't you just stay over? I hate to see you on the roads this late. We got plenty of room. You can leave after breakfast."

—"No, we couldn't do that."

—"There's that double bed in the attic nobody's using."

—"No, then you'd have some more sheets to wash. Can't do it."

—"You'll be fresher in the morning."

—"What do you think, Doris, maybe one night?"

Since you'll be staying the night, you can have another sandwich while you watch Johnny Carson, but when you get tired, don't just stand up and go to bed. Here is the beginning of the Minnesota Long Goodnight:

—"[*Yawn*] Boy, I tell you a guy gets tired."

—"You said it, I'm not gonna last much longer at this rate."

—"Well, if it's all the same to you, then, I think maybe I'll just hit the hay."

In the following dialogue a couple we'll call Bob and Kate are about to leave the home of Harold and Phyllis, where they have stayed overnight. They may have been there two or three days, I don't know. Try your hand at all the parts for practice.

The good-bye begins in the living room on a Saturday afternoon. Nobody is moving toward the door, the coats are still in the closet. Everybody is seated.

BOB: "I think maybe Kate and I are gonna head out then . . ."

HAROLD: "Well, you don't have to rush off, you know, we still got Sunday."

KATE: "We really meant to leave last night, Phyllis."

PHYLLIS: "You guys aren't leaving because of that bed we put you on, are you? Harold and I like a soft mattress."

BOB: "It wasn't too bad, really, but it's a creeper. If you thrash around, it tends to inch across the floor."

HAROLD: "It's always done that. One of these days I've got to nail it down. I'm gonna bracket the legs with two-by-fours, I think."

BOB: "That would do it. I finally blocked it with my shoes so we could get some sleep."

KATE: "Let's go, Bob. Get up off the couch."

PHYLLIS: "Oh, I hate to see you go. Why don't you stay for a little lunch."

BOB: "We just ate an hour ago, Kate."

PHYLLIS: "Well, be that way. At least I'm gonna make up a food bag for you to take in the car. Baloney sandwiches, and a few of the Seven Dwarf Rainbow Bars."

KATE: "You don't have to do that, Phyllis."

HAROLD: "Yes, she does. We're not gonna let you out the door unless you take a little lunch with you. What if your car breaks down?"

The next stage of any Long Good-bye generally takes place in another room of the house. In this dialogue, the scene is Harold and Phyllis's kitchen. Both couples have their coats on and are standing near the door.

BOB: "So okay then, we're leaving now. This is it."

HAROLD: "I still say, you don't have to go on our account. You sure you're not mad about something?"

KATE: "Oh, don't be ridiculous, Harold."

PHYLLIS: "You got the lunch, don't you?"

KATE: "I sure do, Phyllis, but what's in this big Tupperware container?"

PHYLLIS: "It's the rest of that Norwegian Taco salad. Gwen brought it over, remember?"

HAROLD: "Yeah, what makes it special is those pickled herring chunks in it. Boy, can she cook. Give 'em some of that Glorified Rice, too, Phyllis. We got a ton of it."

BOB: "No, we can't take all your food."

PHYLLIS: "You'll be doing us a favor."

KATE: "Well, maybe a little."

HAROLD: "Give 'em a lot."

PHYLLIS: "We'll walk out with you."

BOB: "You don't have to do that."

KATE: "We already got our coats on."

HAROLD: "Don't like our company, or what?"

The next stage of the Long Good-bye takes place outdoors, near the host's house. In this dialogue, both couples are on the lawn. The car has not been started yet.

PHYLLIS: "So you got everything then, Kate?"

KATE: "If we don't have it, we can bring it next time."

BOB: "Kate, we're moving toward the car now. This is it."

HAROLD: "Doesn't that front tire of yours look a little low, Bob? I don't know if I'd take off with a tire like that."

In the finale of the Long Good-bye, the departees are in the car and the hosts are at the open driver's window, bent over. The motor is running.

HAROLD: "Sure you don't want to come back in and have a little lunch before you go? This is your last chance."

BOB: "Nope. We'll be lucky to get home for the 10 o'clock news as it is . . . so thanks for everything then, Harold."

HAROLD: "No problem."

PHYLLIS: "Call us when you get there, will you, Kate?"

KATE: "You bet."

BOB: "I'm letting the clutch out. The car is rolling."

HAROLD: "Bob, what's that ticking noise. Hear it?"

BOB: "It does that when it's cold. Lifters, I'd say."

HAROLD: "Could be the throw-out bearing, though. I don't know, maybe you better stay over. You never know what could happen. It could even be rod bearings."

BOB: "Nope, we're off. We're not stopping for anything. Take it easy."

HAROLD: "Yeah, well, you too then."

PHYLLIS: "Come back."

KATE: "You bet."

As you pull away toward the road, your hosts will wave. You should wave back. The waving should continue until you can no longer see each other. A couple of toots on the horn are optional but always in good taste and much appreciated.

If you forgot something and have to return, the first three stages are optional for the second Long Good-bye, but the conversation out the driver's window is mandatory.

Howard Mohr

THE MINNESOTA QUANTUM GOOD-BYE: AN UPDATE

This last and most important Minnesota lesson needs no major changes for use by visitors from out of state in 2012 and beyond, though minor adjustments would be obvious, such as the reference to watching Johnny Carson before retiring, if you decide to stay overnight and do the Long Good-bye the next day. Otherwise, there it is, the Minnesota Long Good-bye (MLG) the way it has been for years and the way it will be for years to come. Minnesotans are not as effusive as they could be, I suppose, in saying hello, and do fall short on the greeting hugs and air kisses so popular on the East Coast, but Minnesotans are very good at the Long Good-bye. I would be so bold as to say that learning the Minnesota Long Good-bye is more important to a visitor than learning how to accept food only on the third offer.

The Minnesota Long Good-bye incorporates so much of the Minnesota language and character that it can stand alone as an iconic snapshot of what it takes to be Minnesotan. I have participated in many Minnesota Long Good-byes, both as host and as guest, and every time when I get to the last stage of the MLG, where I drive off and give the obligatory two quick toots on the horn and do the backward wave at our hosts, it feels less like a good-bye and more like a hello. It is a very emotional moment, and a guy has to resist the urge to go back and stay another day or two. On the other hand, when I stand by the sidewalk as host and watch our guests depart, I start missing them immediately.

That said, I feel obligated to mention a study that the University of Minnesota Physics Department conducted on the Minnesota Long Good-bye. The research was funded by a grant from the Hotdish Foundation and the Raw Bits Foundation. Professor Krolnjikt took it upon himself to use a stopwatch to accurately time and log a multitude of Minnesota Long Good-byes statewide in order to get a range of data. At the end of a tedious two years of research, Professor Krolnjikt presented his colleagues at the U with a short refresher description of the Long Good-bye from its initiation with that lunge from the chair of the visiting husband and his announcement of "I suppose we oughta be going, then," and the little sack lunch in case the guests got hungry on the drive, and the walk to the vehicle, and the rolling down of the driver's window, and the talking about the possible misfiring spark plugs or the oil leak, and a quick look under the hood to figure out what the squeaking sound was, and finally putting the car in gear and driving away with a couple of good-bye toots and a backward wave.

There were shakes of the heads of the physics professors and at least one finger of a young physicist from Cal Tech twirling around his temple after Dr. Krolnjikt finished his generic account of the Minnesota Long Good-bye. One of them actually said bluntly: "Why are you telling us this?" Chairs were starting to scrape. That's when Dr. Krolnjikt threw them the bombshell:

"No matter when the Minnesota Long Good-bye started or when the last toot on the horn echoed, EVERY ONE OF THOSE LONG GOOD-BYES TOOK EXACTLY THE SAME AMOUNT OF TIME, DOWN TO THE SECOND."

Dr. Krolnjikt told his colleagues that he was not able to increase or decrease the speed of the Long Good-bye with any sort of external influence. Dr. Krolnjikt's data was accepted as probationary proof that the Minnesota Long Good-bye was indeed a quantum phenomenon. The speed of light never varies. It turns out that the speed of the Minnesota Long Good-bye also never varies, and is therefore, like the speed of light, a universal constant.

This explains for me the strange, apparent simultaneity of a Minnesota Long Good-bye feeling like a wonderful hello, though I wonder if Dr. Krolnjikt would agree.